1992

The Year That Shaped the World We Live In

MATTHEW R. SMITH

Copyright © 2025 *Matthew R. Smith*

Published by CaryPress International Books
www.CaryPress.com

All rights reserved. No part of this publication may be reproduced, distributed, or transmitted in any form or by any means, including photocopying, recording, or other electronic or mechanical methods, without the prior written permission of the publisher, except in the case of brief quotations embodied in critical reviews and certain other non-commercial uses permitted by copyright law.

For Mom and Dad

Table of Contents

Foreword 1

Chapter 1: A Cold War Melts/ An Empire Ends/ A New Russia 3

Chapter 2: 3's A Party: The 1992 Presidential Campaign 39

Chapter 3: The Seattle Sonic Boom and the Riff Heard Round the World 73

Chapter 4: Bosnia and Somalia: Peacekeeping Missions and The UN
    Post-Cold War 109

Chapter 5: Rodney King, Race & Society 145

Chapter 6: The World Over: Earth Summit in Rio, Free Trade, etc. 189

Afterwards 209

Bibliography 211

Foreword

The inspiration for this book is quite simple. For most of my life I have enjoyed reading and learning history. The personalities, the events and the context of the times in which they took place have always had a special appeal for me. To read about a person or event is often more than just that single subject. It is also about the time in which they took place, which also entails popular culture, politics and so much more. It's almost the same as a good novel, but the events and people described in it are real.

Regarding the 1992, it is a story of a time that I felt deserved to be remembered, even celebrated. The events, the changes, the politics, and especially the music. No matter how much time has passed between now and then, it will be forever remembered as the year the world literally shook and the foundations for the world we live was laid. In many ways, the world has never moved on from 1992. There is still one superpower, there is still a debate that rages about nationalism and protectionism, there is still racial strife, and there is still no one genre that has burst onto the scene and had as much influence as the Grunge Movement. Thirty-three years is a long time, yet in some ways it is not long at all.

I was only ten years old in 1992, and although I do remember most of the events contained within these pages, at the time they barely registered since I was so young. As I got older, I wanted to do more than just read and learn. I wanted to contribute to the narrative that is the ever-changing pantheon of Human and World History. This subject was one that I felt had not been addressed in its totality. This book, while it does not cover every significant event that happened in 1992, I feel it does do justice to addressing the major ones that not only grabbed headlines but changed the world and us.

I hope that in expressing the thoughts within this book, I will tell a story and address a subject that educates, entertains and inspires. Its intended audience is any and everyone intrigued by its subject matter. It is not intended to be overly statistical, although facts and figures are necessary to tell the story, but to try and tell of these events in a way that (hopefully) appeals to everyone. I hope this story has that intended effect and I hope you enjoy it!

CHAPTER 1

A Cold War Melts
An Empire Ends
A New Russia

On December 25, 1991, the flag of the U.S.S.R. (Soviet Union) was lowered over the iKremlin for the last time and raised in its place was the flag of the Russian Federation. After just sixty-nine years of existence, the Soviet Union had ceased to be. Its fifteen Republics would all become independent nations and choose their own destiny. Earlier that day, Mikhail Gorbachev had resigned as General Secretary of the Communist Party, and the President of the Soviet Union was to be replaced with Russian President Boris Yeltsin. The speed and sudden collapse had taken everyone in the world by surprise.

Throughout history, many empires have lasted much longer than the Soviet Union. A few examples, such as the Romans, Persians, Ottomans, or the Holy Roman Empire, come to mind. However, none of those entities were able to end all life on Earth or had the global and ideological reach that the Soviets did at their height. All of that was suddenly gone. The East-West confrontation of nearly half a century simply ceased to be, and there was only one superpower, which was the United States. What came next is still playing out to this day.

It seems hard to fathom now that after forty-years of brinkmanship and near catastrophe (Cuban Missile Crisis) that the division of the world into two camps, communist and non-communist, just simply ended in December 1991 with almost no bloodshed and not a shot fired. The capitalistic west led by the United States which championed free markets, civil liberties and elective democracy had decisively beaten the command economies/ dictatorship of the Soviet Union. Instead of going out with a bang and a world war, the Communists Eastern Bloc nations simply collapsed under the weight of their own system. This was nothing short of a miraculous development considering that for over four decades since the end of World War II, the two sides had been at each other's throats in every way imaginable. From a divided Germany and its capital Berlin, to fighting each other through proxy wars in third world countries such as Korea and Vietnam coming foremost to mind, to outright confrontation (Berlin Airlift and the Cuban Missile crisis). Families all over the world dreaded and lived with the threat of nuclear war and built underground shelters.

Perhaps it could be stated that the beginning of the end of the Soviet Union and communism can be traced to two events in 1979. The first is the appointment of John Paul II from Communist Poland as the new Pope, and the second is the invasion of Afghanistan later that year. It could be argued that the ascension of John Paul II was a spiritual blow to the Communists and that the invasion of Afghanistan by the Soviet Union was the beginning of its physical destruction, although the arms build-up of the Reagan years would also play a role in this.

The consequences of the collapse of the Soviet Union would produce effects that would last long after the year of 1992 and have a much broader meaning than the collapse of Communism and the end of the Cold War. Instead of two superpowers, there was now only one. Although democracy and free markets reigned supreme, the world would hardly be at peace, and it would certainly not be, as Francis Fukuyama said, "The end of history." Fukuyama said himself, "What we may be witnessing is not just the end of the Cold War, or the passing of a particular period of post-war history, but the end of history as such: that is, the end point of mankind's ideological evolution and the universalization of Western liberal democracy as the final form of human government." Although it is undeniable that Fukuyama's statement has come to pass in many quarters, such as Eastern Europe, it remains to be seen whether this will be the case in most of the third world, such as Africa, Latin America, and the Middle East. One thing, however, is certain: the end of the Cold War did not signal the end of history, and the world we now live in is, if anything, extremely fractured and less safe. In place of superpower confrontation, we have rogue third-world countries attempting to gain nuclear technology, as well as ethnic, sectarian violence and genocide (Rwanda and the Balkans) or mass starvation and failed states (Somalia).

As much as the collapse of the Soviet Union would change the world, an almost equally titanic struggle would be waged to bring democracy and free markets to the new Russian Federation practically overnight. The results would be mixed and the consequences far-reaching, especially for the Russian people. Russia's transition to democracy would not be smooth, and as we can see today, it would not bring about liberal representative democracy in the Western sense. Still, communism was gone, and it was not coming back. What lay ahead as 1992 dawned on the new Federation of Russia was a tug of war as it sought to build a new future while trying to rid itself of its recent authoritarian past.

Throughout the 1980s, the people of the Soviet Union had become increasingly restless. The country had been bogged down in a losing war in Afghanistan for almost a decade, with little to show for it but mounting casualties. Food and goods shortages resulted in empty store shelves as Russians waited in long lines for what little grocery items and consumer goods that were available. The old dogmas and ideologies of class warfare, as well as socialist brotherhood, rang hollow and meant little to ordinary Russians and those throughout the U.S.S.R. At the start of the decade, the Soviet Union was ruled by the increasingly senile and reclusive Leonid Brezhnev, who had come to power in 1964 after ousting Nikita Khrushchev as First General Secretary of the Communist Party. He passed away from a heart attack on November 10, 1982, at the age of seventy-five, to be replaced by Yuri Andropov, who only held power for fifteen months before he too died on February 9, 1984, of kidney failure at the age of sixty-nine. Andropov's successor was Constantine Chernenko, who also ruled for fifteen months before dying due to various health issues on March 10, 1985, at age seventy-three. In only two and a half years, three Soviet leaders had passed away, leading President Ronald Reagan to famously quip, "How am I supposed to get anywhere with the Soviets if they keep dying on me?" The next General Secretary would not only be a complete break from the past, but would be someone who would be able to bring about great changes in concert with Western leaders, not in spite of them. It was obvious from the start that Mikhail Sergeyevich Gorbachev was unlike any previous General Secretaries of the Soviet Union the world had ever seen. For starters, he was relatively young, coming to power at age fifty-four, making it much more likely that he would not die in office like his immediate predecessors.

Born on March 2, 1931, Gorbachev worked his way up the Communist Party hierarchy from an early age via the Komsomol organization and was aided by his family's proletarian background. Throughout his long career with the party, Gorbachev always had an independent streak that he managed to conceal over the years. He harbored doubts about the 1968 Soviet invasion of Czechoslovakia yet supported it publicly. Throughout the 1970 s, he and his wife, Raisa, visited Western Europe on several occasions, during which he found himself questioning the efficiency of the Soviet system when he saw how easily citizens of France and Germany spoke their minds and criticized their leaders without fear of imprisonment. Starting in 1979, the Soviet Union would begin to suffer a series of very poor harvests, forcing them to import more grain from abroad, leading Gorbachev to question the efficiency of collectivized agriculture. Finally, Gorbachev believed that the 1979 invasion of Afghanistan was a grave mistake that should not have happened, even though he publicly supported it. Despite these misgivings, Gorbachev remained committed to the ideals of Socialism, the Russian revolution, and wisely, was not too outspoken with his doubts. As the 1970 s came to a close, Gorbachev came to believe that serious reforms would be needed if the Soviet Union was to remain a world power on par with the United States.

By the time of General Secretary Constantine Chernenko's death in March 1985, Gorbachev had become a powerful figure within the government as a full-fledged member of the Politburo since October 1980, as well as having already been on the Central Committee since 1978 as a Secretariat for Agriculture. At this point, he was well positioned within the government to be able to start pursuing some reforms. When Yuri Andropov had passed away the previous February, Gorbachev had been considered a successor but it was felt that at only fifty-three he was too young and not ready to be General Secretary yet. With the no less sudden passing of Constantine Chernenko only thirteen months later, Gorbachev's youth suddenly became an asset and he was selected as the eighth General Secretary of the Communist Party of the Soviet Union on March 11, 1985. It was obvious from the start that Gorbachev intended to introduce serious reforms. Yet, in order to do so, he had to be sure not to offend the Central Committee or the Politburo, both of whom could remove him from the office. Ironically, as time went on he would also have to contend with several party hardliners who felt his reforms went too far and Liberals who felt they didn't go far enough.

The two main reforms associated with Gorbachev during his tenure were the now well-known Glasnost and Perestroika. The former meaning openness and the latter, restructuring when translated to English. Glasnost was the relaxing of restrictions on free speech and debate that had been commonplace in the Soviet Union all throughout its existence. It was hoped that by giving people a chance to debate and express themselves freely without fear of imprisonment, that the country could find solutions to its pressing problems. Perestroika was about restructuring the way the highly centralized Soviet state and economy functioned by relaxing regulations and giving more autonomy to local and regional authorities. A major component of this was allowing all the various ministries to conduct trade with foreign entities without having to deal with the Ministry of Foreign Trade. Perestroika also allowed for the ownership of private business in certain sectors of the economy such as food and retail. It is important to note that even though Soviet citizens gained more freedom than they ever previously had, these reforms were not constitutional guarantees of any sort and could be reversed at any time.

While affecting change and reform at home, Gorbachev was also making huge strides abroad. From November 1985 to May 1988, Gorbachev and U.S. President Ronald Reagan met on four occasions and made great progress in easing the tensions of the Cold War, which had risen sharply during Reagan's first term in office (1981-1985). The capstone of these summits would be the Intermediate Nuclear Forces (INF) treaty that was signed in Washington, D.C. on December 8, 1987, and ratified by both countries the following May. Gorbachev also intended to withdraw Soviet forces from the war in Afghanistan, which had been a consistent drain on the country's resources since its beginning in December 1979. Although it would take several years before the withdrawal would begin earnestly in mid-1988, Gorbachev had intended to do so since he came to power in March 1985. Foreign aid to Socialist allies in the Eastern Bloc had also heavily taxed Soviet funds. At the time of Gorbachev's ascension to the General Secretariat, the rest of the Communist Bloc received an estimated $17 billion in raw goods, while the U.S.S.R. itself was only taking in $3-5 billion in return. (Taubman, 2017. p. 267) Although he disdained anything resembling a cult of personality, Gorbachev had become a rock star of sorts in the West, where he was seen as an earnest liberal reformer.

In many aspects, Gorbachev's reforms and leadership could be seen as a major success. Cold War tensions had significantly decreased with friendly and productive dialogues with Western leaders, particularly President Reagan and then President Bush. As a result of Glasnost, Soviet citizens from all walks of life (particularly journalists and academics) were beginning to re-evaluate their past and debate whether Communism was the best course of action for the country's future. Due to Perestroika, local officials and businessmen did not have to deal as much with the central government when running their agencies or businesses. The most visible sign of this would be the opening of the first ever McDonald's, the famous American fast-food chain, on January 31, 1990, in Pushkin square Moscow.

The flip side of all the progress made by Gorbachev's reforms would also be the profound consequences for the future of the Soviet state. In much the same way that the collapse of Communism fueled the nationalism of the Yugoslav Republics in the Balkans, the reforms in the

U.S.S.R. also contributed to growing restlessness and nationalism among not only the Soviet Republics, but Eastern European Bloc countries as well. Beginning with the fall of the Berlin Wall in East Germany in November 1989, countries that had been part of the Warsaw Pact (a Cold War alliance of Eastern European nations) began to hold elections and throw off the yoke of Communism. The same thing began to occur in not only the Republics (Ukraine, Belarus, Estonia, Latvia, Lithuania, etc.) but Russia itself when, on June 12, 1990, the Russian Soviet Federative Socialist Republic (RSFSR) declared its sovereignty, although still part of the Soviet Union. It was during this time that a man already prominent within the Communist Party and the nation began to increasingly take center stage in the public consciousness. It was also he who would play the central role in trying to bring democracy and capitalism to the soon-to-be-born Russian Federation in the seismic changes and titanic struggles of 1992.

Boris Nikolayevich Yeltsin was born on February 1, 1931, ironically just one month before Gorbachev, in Sverdlovsk Oblast to a family of poor farmers. Yeltsin started work in the construction industry as a builder and engineer upon graduating from the Ural Polytechnic Institute in 1955. Unlike Gorbachev, Yeltsin was not politically inclined and was only active in the Communist Party as a matter of necessity for career advancement. When Yeltsin actively sought membership in the party in 1960, he had to omit the fact that his grandfather was a Kulak, which was a land owning class of wealthy farmers who were persecuted and exiled by Soviet authorities during the collectivization of agriculture in the 1930s. Fortunately for Yeltsin, his true family history was not revealed until he became President of the Russian Federation many years later.

Yeltsin's career progressed with him leading several large building projects, being promoted and moving up the party hierarchy. Yeltsin's managerial skills became fine-tuned as he supervised a variety of large building projects with an ever-larger number of workers under him which attracted the attention of regional party officials in the Sverdlovsk Oblast. Throughout the 1960 s and 70 s, Yeltsin steadily moved up within the ranks of the regional party infrastructure. In 1976, he was appointed First Secretary of the Party Committee for Sverdlovsk Oblast which involved being interviewed by General Secretary Leonid Brezhnev himself. During his years as First Secretary in Sverdlovsk, Yeltsin gained valuable experience in several areas of national policy. It was also during this time that he honed and perfected his political skills in dealing with the Soviet public at large. He would become known for making impromptu visits all over the Oblast, as well as his attention to detail about issues dealing with quality of life. He would work to build new roads, bridges, schools and even a subway system. In one famous speech, he held a question-and-answer session with students at the Sverdlovsk Youth Palace in May 1981, where he gave a speech and talked openly about problems within the Oblast. He also held a question-and-answer session with the audience which was made up mostly of youths.

While First Secretary of Sverdlovsk, Yeltsin also had greater exposure to national politics and, like Gorbachev, began to have doubts about the Soviet system and felt that it was in need of serious reform. His open and frank discussions did not sit well with some in the party hierarchy, yet no action was taken against him. In April 1985, after Gorbachev became General Secretary, Yeltsin was appointed as head of the Construction Department of the Party's Central Committee and moved to Moscow. Eight months later in December 1985, Gorbachev promoted Yeltsin to General Secretary of the Moscow Communist Party. This position would make Yeltsin responsible for all aspects of the city's management and basically made him a de facto mayor. The same managerial attention to detail that he had shown in Sverdlovsk as an engineer and First Secretary, were once again put to use addressing the capital city's problems.

As before, Yeltsin was not afraid to speak his mind in trying to get things done. Upon taking office, Yeltsin fired 90% of the city administrators. As he had done during his days as First Secretary in Sverdlovsk, Yeltsin would walk the streets and talk with Muscovites from all walks of life and loudly complain about the failures of the party. Even more galling to the party was his exposure of perks that party members enjoyed that were not available to regular citizens, such as spouses of party officials being chauffeured to special stores and their children being given preferential treatment in being admitted to universities. (Taubman, 2017. p. 324) It was during this time that Yeltsin's relationship with Gorbachev began to seriously deteriorate. Yeltsin had always had a hot and cold relationship with Gorbachev. Despite both men being strong advocates for reform, they butted heads time and again throughout Yeltsin's two and one-half years in Moscow before he resigned from the Politburo. Gorbachev found Yeltsin too outspoken, too emotional, and often insubordinate, while Yeltsin felt that Gorbachev's reforms were moving too slowly. Yeltsin also found Gorbachev to be condescending and arrogant. One trait of Gorbachev's that particularly grated on Yeltsin was his habit of addressing his subordinates with ty (used in the second person singular) as opposed to the more proper vy Yeltsin preferred. (Taubman, 2017. p. 322) However, given the historical situation and the position both men were in, it was inevitable that a confrontation between them would happen in the near future.

The final break between the two men occurred on October 21, 1987, when Yeltsin openly criticized Gorbachev at a Central Committee meeting about how problems he brought to the attention of his superiors and Gorbachev were not being addressed. Yeltsin had attempted to resign from the Politburo the previous month due to these frustrations. Never before had a Soviet official spoken to a General Secretary in such a manner, and its effect was shocking. This was also the first time that someone had attempted to resign from the Politburo. The stress on Yeltsin became so bad that he was hospitalized after cutting himself in an apparent suicide attempt a few weeks later on November 10. The next day, on November 11, Gorbachev had scheduled a meeting of Moscow's city party in order to decide Yeltsin's fate, who was still recovering from his self-inflicted wounds at a hospital in the city. At the meeting, Yeltsin had to endure being berated with torrents of abuse from fellow party members who all regurgitated stock phrases of disapproval for hours while Yeltsin sat silently. It was character assassination and verbal abuse typical of the show trials in the Stalin era. Yeltsin would never forget, nor forgive Gorbachev for such harrowing treatment. Yeltsin was then formally fired as First Secretary of the Moscow Communist Party. Shortly afterwards, Yeltsin was demoted to the position of First Deputy Commissioner for the State Committee for Construction.

Throughout 1988, Yeltsin would remain in exile and recover from his wounds both physically and politically. With good cause, he believed that he was finished in national politics and wanted to remain alone and in peace. Ironically, his greatest rival would be instrumental in his return and ultimate triumph. Faced with an obstructionist conservative element opposed to his reforms, Gorbachev created the Congress of the People's Deputies, a new legislative body that would hopefully reform the Supreme Soviet, at the nineteenth party conference in July 1988. The election of the new deputies would be held on March 26, 1989. Having been encouraged by liberal stalwarts and those in favor of abolishing communism altogether, Yeltsin ran and won election as a delegate for the district of Moscow. Out of 5,722,937 votes cast, Yeltsin won 5,238,206 votes for a whopping 91.53% of the vote compared to his rival's paltry 393,633 votes and just 6.88 %. (Aron. p. 275. 2000) The Deputies then in turn elected him to a seat within the Supreme Soviet two months later. Almost a year later, Yeltsin would be elected as a delegate from his home region of Sverdlovsk.

At this juncture, the political situation within the Soviet Union and Eastern Europe was moving at a breakneck pace. The Berlin Wall was torn down in November 1989, and dissidents who had spoken out against Soviet rule were gaining political power across the Eastern Bloc. Most notably, Vaclav Havel in Czechoslovakia (Dec. 1989) and Lech Walesa in Poland (Dec. 1990) respectively. Meanwhile, back in the Soviet Union, a combination of radical and anti-communist supporters within the new Supreme Soviet helped propel Yeltsin first to the Chairmanship in May 1990 and then finally, to the Presidency of the Russian Soviet Federative Socialist Republic (RSFSR) in July 1991. The presidential election was a resounding victory for Yeltsin, who won with 58.56% of ballots cast for 45,552,042 votes to just 17.22% and 13,359,335 for his opponent, Nikolai Ryzhkov, who was Gorbachev's hand-picked candidate and ran as a Communist. (Aron, p.434, 2000) Yeltsin himself had, in typical dramatic fashion, already publicly resigned from the Communist Party of the Soviet Union in May 1990.

Discontent among Communist hardliners had been growing for several years as Gorbachev's reforms began to bring about change. From August 18-21, 1991, a cadre of high-level officials, mainly under the direction of Soviet Vice President Gennady Yanayev, launched a coup d'etat against both Gorbachev and Yeltsin. Gorbachev had been vacationing at his Dacha in the Crimea and was basically put under house arrest, while Yeltsin managed to evade capture. Forces loyal to the coup leaders also took up positions around Moscow. It was during these three days of uncertainty that saw Yeltsin's finest hour, when on August 19, 1991, he stood atop a tank outside the White House (the Russian Parliament building) and, raising a megaphone, called for citizens to reject the coup and for Gorbachev to be freed. He began by saying, "The peoples of Russia are becoming masters of their destiny. The uncontrolled powers of unconstitutional organs have been considerably limited, and this includes party organs." Next, he tore into the coup plotters by proclaiming, "We are dealing with a rightist, reactionary, anti-constitutional coup. Despite all the difficulties and severe trials being experienced by the people, the democratic process in the country is acquiring an increasingly broad sweep and an irreversible character." Then, in closing, he stated, "We appeal to citizens of Russia to give a fitting rebuff to the putschists and demand a return of the country to normal constitutional development." (Yeltsin's Speech) It made for a powerful and riveting scene that resonated far and wide across the world. The first democratically elected president of a newly independent Russia was standing up to would-be tyrants trying to turn back the clock and risking his life. Not until almost a decade later, when President George W. Bush stood on the ruins of the World Trade Center after the terrorist attacks of September 11, 2001, did a world leader project such a vivid image of defiance and resolve. Yet, even then, President Bush was not in any physical danger as Yeltsin very much was. The coup collapsed on August 22, and Gorbachev was returned to power, although his position and authority were significantly weakened.

Perhaps nothing signaled the changes sweeping the Soviet Union in a cultural sense than when on September 28, 1991, the Monsters of Rock, a heavy metal music festival, was held outside Moscow at Tushino airfield. Several high-profile acts such as the Black Crowes, AC/DC, Pantera, and most notably, Metallica, performed for a massive crowd of 1.6 million

Russian metal fans. Uniformed Soviet guards stood watch as the crowd raged to the tunes of their favorite heavy metal bands. Just a few years, or even months ago, such a festival happening would have been unthinkable. It was a testament to the ongoing success of Glasnost and Gorbachev's reforms that the country had gotten to this point.

From the declaration of Russian Sovereignty in June 1990, to the proposed new union treaty which gave the Republics more autonomy and power (ironically due to be signed on the date of the August 1991 coup attempt) and finally the Belavezha Accords (which declared the U.S.S.R defunct between Russia, Ukraine and Belarus on December 8, 1991), the writing on the wall could not be clearer. For all intents and purposes, the Soviet Union had already ceased to exist. Finally, on December 24, 1991, the end came when Gorbachev agreed to formally resign his office as General Secretary of the U S.S.R. and dissolve the nation altogether in a nationally televised speech. Throughout the speech, Gorbachev recounted all his achievements from Perestroika, Glasnost and the various arms control agreements that were signed. Despite all that had been accomplished, he cautioned that the country still had a long way to go stating, "This society acquired freedom, liberated itself politically and spiritually, and this is the foremost achievement which we have not yet understood completely, because we have not learned to use freedom." He celebrated the demise of the totalitarian state and extolled the virtues of private property ownership and a market economy. He proclaimed, "We live in a new world. The Cold War has ended, the arms race has stopped, as has the insane militarization which mutilated our economy, public psyche and morals. The threat of a world war has been removed." Also recounted was the struggle to bring about change, stating of his reforms, " They were carried out with sharp struggle, with growing resistance from the old, the obsolete forces: the former party-state structures, the economic apparatus, as well as our habits, ideological superstitions, the psychology of sponging and leveling everyone out." (Mikhail Gorbachev). Yet, he also expressed disappointment that this was the end point of all his policies of reform as well as the fact that Russia was in for hard times ahead. Gorbachev had wanted to reform the Socialist system, not bring about its downfall. This perhaps being the greatest irony of all.

The point of no return had been passed, and the downfall of the world's first Communist nation was complete. For sixty-nine years, the ideologies of Marx, Engels and Lennin had been fully instituted with five-year plans, purges, collectivization, and famines resulting in endless mounds of millions of corpses. Now that experiment has irrevocably failed. The Soviet Union was gone, never to return. As 1992 dawned, the Russian people were filled with great hope and anxiety about what the new future would bring. For years, Gorbachev and Yeltsin were locked in a death struggle between the old and the new. Although both men were reformers and had much in common, it was Yeltsin who prevailed in the end and would now lead the Russian Federation into this new world and era. As events as would show shortly, he had his work more than cut out for him.

As 1992 began, President Yeltsin faced a task of monumental complexity and difficulty. First and foremost, Yeltsin had to secure the Soviet Union's vast nuclear arsenal that was spread out among several now independent republics. He then had to shift Russia's economy from a state-controlled command one, to one of free markets and private ownership / investment. This alone would be a massive undertaking requiring an entire re-ordering of the relationship between business and state as well as foreign entities. With no historical precedent to draw on in Russian history, Yeltsin was starting from scratch. Next, Yeltsin, and Russia's elected officials, had to build the foundations of a modern democratic state. In order to accomplish this, he would need to establish a productive working relationship with the Supreme Soviet of Russia and The Congress of the People's Deputies, the two legislative bodies now governing the Russian Federation. As will be discussed shortly, that relationship had yet to be established. Finally, Russia's relationship with the world and the United States would be completely redefined. Boris Yeltsin, the former construction manager and engineer, was now expected to build a new Russia and quickly.

Now that the Cold War was over and the threat of nuclear war between the superpowers was gone, it was of paramount importance that the former Soviet Union's nuclear arsenal be secured and safely disposed of. The threat of these weapons either falling into the wrong hands or leaking radiation due to improper handling and other maintenance related issues, was a major source of concern throughout the whole world. To accomplish this, it was necessary that a productive working relationship be established with the President of the United States, George H.W. Bush. Shortly after he became President of the RSFSR in June 1991, Yeltsin had visited Washington, D.C. and officially met with Bush. At the time Bush had to walk a delicate position between trying to start a positive relationship with the man likely to succeed Gorbachev, while at the same time not undermining the General Secretary.

Almost immediately, as 1992 began, Yeltsin began reaching out to the Bush administration, eager to reach new arms reduction agreements as well as requesting aid for housing dismantled nuclear warheads. In early February, Bush hosted Yeltsin at the President's retreat at Camp David, M.D. where the two men signed a formal statement declaring that the Cold War was over and that the relationship between the two countries would characterize by "friendship and partnership". Both men seemed to get on quite well with one another and were soon on a first name basis.

Bush felt good about Yeltsin's intentions, and Yeltsin, in turn, was very impressed by Bush and his knowledge of foreign policy. Although no concrete decisions were made, both men agreed on the need to reduce their respective nuclear arsenals with Yeltsin proposing that both countries trim the number of warheads each possesses down to 2,500. (Wines, Feb 2, 1992) This first visit was a major boost for Yeltsin and gave him much-needed prestige at home and abroad. As much as Yeltsin wanted to be seen as an equal of the United States, he also knew that he would have to depend on them for any large amounts of foreign aid of which there would be a great deal over the coming years. Fortunately for Russia and the rest of the world as well, two United States Senators had shown great foresight regarding nuclear proliferation regarding the soon-to-be defunct Soviet Union's arsenal. Indiana Republican Richard Lugar and Georgia Democrat Sam Nunn had authored The Soviet Nuclear Threat Reduction Act of 1991, or what would come to be simply known as Lugar-Nunn. Signed into law by President Bush on December 12, 1991, Luger-Nunn sought to provide direct aid and assistance to Russia and several former republics in the transportation and deactivation of its nuclear weapons, as well as the conversion of nuclear materials for civilian use. The Cooperative Threat Reduction program established by Lugar-Nunn would be an ongoing effort to denuclearize the former republics and keep non-state actors from acquiring them or their technology.

In October 1991, The Supreme Soviet of Russia had granted President Yeltsin the extraordinary power to rule to by decree. These emergency powers would give Yeltsin practically dictatorial power to govern and reform Russia as he saw fit. Yeltsin's reforms would often be referred to as "shock therapy". The man credited with advocating and putting these policies into action would be one Yegor Gaidar who served as Yeltsin's Finance Minister for five pivotal months from November

1991-April 1992. Gaidar would wear many hats in the Yeltsin administration, serving as acting Prime Minister from June - December, while at the same time filling the position of Deputy Prime Minister from March - December. Although he had Yeltsin's confidence as an accomplished academic and economist, Gaidar would come to symbolize the conflict and discord between Yeltsin and the Supreme Soviet / Congress of People's Deputies that would worsen throughout the year and eventually poison relations between the two branches of government. Still, it was Gaidar who by and large was the intellectual architect of Yeltsin's shock therapy economic policies. As 1992 would show, shock is definitely what his policies produced. Although therapy would be debatable, they certainly brought about radical change for all of Russia.

In a series of far-reaching decrees, Yeltsin single-handedly, and almost overnight, sought to convert Russia from the old command economy of the Soviet Union to one based on the free market capitalism of the West. Private businesses and other enterprises were allowed to form as well as trade with foreign entities with much less interference from the state due to Decree #65 issued on January 29, which was titled "On Freedom of Trade". This was accomplished via a process called "Voucher Privatization" whereby land and business owners were given a state certificate signifying that they now had full ownership of their assets and property. The vouchers, which were widely distributed among the general population, also served to allow everyday citizens to buy stock and take a share of ownership in previously state-controlled businesses. Long-standing price controls were also abolished in an effort to reduce shortages of the goods and services that had been so prevalent during the last years of the Soviet Union.

As a result of these reforms, 90% of retail and 80% of wholesale prices would no longer be subjected to state control and would now be dependent on the laws of supply and demand. (Colton, p. 228, 2008) In the sectors of agriculture and farming, which had borne the brunt of brutal collectivization in the 1920s and 1930s, farms were given the choices of disbanding and dividing up the land, remaining within their current cooperatives, or reorganizing as joint stock companies. Only 7% of 40% of farmers polled favored retaining the collective farming system. (Ellison, p. 179, 2006) In Yeltsin's words, the goal was to "unloose prices, that is to introduce a real market forcefully and roughly the way [Russian landlords and peasants] were ordered to plant potatoes under Peter the Great, and second, to create private property… to create a class of owners." (Colton, p. 226. 2008)

The immediate effect of these reforms, however well intentioned, would prove to be catastrophic for everyday Russians. Although the sudden and abrupt end to price controls had resulted in a flood of consumer goods and the end of shortages, it also triggered massive inflation that decimated Russia's currency, the Ruble, as well as wiped out the savings of many Russian families and businesses. The loose monetary policies of the Russian Central Bank contributed a great deal towards this. With massive amounts of money being printed predictably the value of the currency tanked. In January alone consumer prices rose 296% while inflation would average 2,520% for the year 1992. (Colton, p. 230, 2008) Ironically, many Russians could now no longer afford to buy the items so recently replenished on the shelves of stores and were facing the same hardships under Democratic (some would say nominally) Yeltsin as they did under Communist (albeit reforming) Gorbachev.

A PBS Frontline documentary that aired on February 25, 1992, gave a detailed insight into how the newly privatized businesses and everyday Russians were impacted by the collapse of the Soviet Union and Yeltsin's reforms. To start with, many different industries had longstanding partnerships with companies and factories in the former Republics who were now sovereign counties in their own right. To ship parts, buy, sell or trade now required crossing an international border. This combined with the fact that many former Republics were now either creating their own currency or phasing out the ruble only served to complicate things economically.

An example given of this in the documentary is that of the Uralmash industrial plant, which makes heavy machinery in Yekaterinburg, just west of Siberia in the Sverdlovsk Oblast. PBS investigative journalist Hendrick Smith finds that upon interviewing the acting director of the plant (the director died during filming of a heart attack) that the liberalization of the economy has brought about chaos and disorder instead of profits and prosperity. Under Communist rule, everything from the factory's customers, wages, and output was dictated by the government. While the factory was not allowed to make a profit or choose what it wanted to produce and whom to sell to, the business was nevertheless stable. With the collapse of the Soviet Union and privatization, the plant is unable to procure the parts needed to assemble the machines due to factors such as previous domestic suppliers now being foreign companies. The acting director explains that pipes that are needed in production are stopped at the Ukrainian border and forced to turn around due to the Ukrainian President's policy (which is not elaborated on). The acting director then uses an example of a small condenser that is also necessary in order to build the machines made at the plant but is currently unavailable due to the fact that the Baltic States no longer sell them to the factory. He then deadpans and states, "We have more freedom than we need. But unfortunately, you can't make a condenser out of freedom." (PBS Frontline, 1992) The story of the Uralmash factory clearly shows that the road from communism to capitalism is not as simple as changing policy, permitting free enterprise, and tearing down statues. For Russian businesses and citizens, it has proven to be an extremely complicated process that involves a number of variables that would take time to sort out.

Long before the collapse of the Soviet Union, Yeltsin had been convinced that only radical and systemic change could bring about a shift in the country's standard of living and economy. Yeltsin's first visit to the United States on September 9-17, 1989, had crystallized his belief in this. Like so many of his peers who had never set foot outside of the Soviet Union and only knew of the West as what state propaganda told them, Yeltsin was beyond awestruck at the huge differences in the standard of living between the two countries. Visiting a grocery store in Houston, Texas, Yeltsin simply could not believe the abundance of food and goods available for purchase by ordinary citizens and at such low prices compared to those back home. Even more shocking was his discovery that barcoded scanners in use had 30,000 products inventoried and were capable of storing far more. Crestfallen on his way to his next destination, Yeltsin confided to an advisor that, "They had to deceive the population. And now it is plain why Soviet citizens were not permitted to go abroad. They [the bosses] were afraid that their eyes would be open." Yeltsin would state afterwards this visit had changed his worldview profoundly and made him realize that, "I had been a Communist by Soviet tradition, by inertia, and by upbringing, but not by conviction." (Colton, p. 172. 2008) To bring about the changes needed to get Russia up to first-world standards, speed would be key.

However necessary the change was for the new Russian Federation, one vital component that was missing was the existence of strong regulatory state organs that could mitigate the excesses of a free-market capitalist economy that existed in most Western economies. As a result, simple price-gouging statutes and other commonplace laws were non-existent. Another serious hurdle impacting the market reforms was the Central Bank of Russia. As previously stated, the bank's excess printing of paper currency helped drive the astronomical rate of inflation throughout 1992. Another problem with the bank was that it was not directly controlled by the Executive branch of government but by the Supreme Soviet of Russia, which, unfortunately for Yeltsin, contained hard-liners who were not supportive of his reforms. The director of the Central Bank would at times be an extension of this feud, which was especially the case with the acting director, Viktor Gerashchenko, appointed by Gaidar in July 1992. (Goldman, p. 107, 1994)

The issue with the Central Bank was endemic to a much larger and far more pressing problem that would eventually lead to crises between the two branches of the new Russian government. The relationship between Yeltsin and the Supreme Soviet / Congress of People's Deputies was always contentious and antagonistic at best. As stated previously, Yeltsin had been granted extraordinary but limited powers to rule by decree from the Supreme Soviet of Russia in October 1991. Throughout 1992, the legislative bodies of Russia understandably felt sidelined in light of Yeltsin's reordering of Russian society by decree, and the situation was not helped by what many considered to be Yeltsin's at times patronizing and condescending attitude towards those not in line with his views and agenda. A quote by Russian historian Yurii Burton stated that Yeltsin at times could be patronizing, "...as one would to a child who does not understand his own interests and cannot be allowed to participate in the affairs of state." (Colton, p. 227, 2008) Ironically, most of the criticisms of Yeltsin were the same ones he'd had with Gorbachev.

Two major power figures that would become a thorn in Yeltsin's side were the Vice President of Russia, Alexander Rutskoy and Chairmen of the Supreme Soviet, Ruslan Khasbulatov. Although both men had initially been supporters of Yeltsin during the coup attempt in August 1991, they began to oppose his policies throughout 1992, which in time would escalate into not just political conflict but military as well, resulting in Yeltsin's violent dissolution of Parliament in October 1993. Yet long before then, relations between the three most powerful men in Russia were poisoned beyond repair. A critical episode in this saga was Yeltsin's attempt to appoint Yegor Gaidar as Prime Minister which was obstructed by the Supreme Soviet forcing Yeltsin to appoint him as Acting Prime Minister. Parliamentary opposition to Yeltsin also took the form of adopting resolutions attacking government policies, attempts to rescind or limit Yeltsin's powers by decree and issues of constitutional reform.

One unintended consequence of the reforms was the explosion of organized crime, gangs, and syndicates throughout Russia. Although organized crime and criminal elements existed under the Soviet Union, their influence was severely limited. This was mainly due to the government's control over all aspects of the economy and the lack of private ownership. With the privatization of the markets and the collapse of state regulatory and policing organs, many new businesses found themselves susceptible to extortion and blackmail by various criminal elements that demanded "protection" money. Violence and intimidation by gangs and individuals were the methods by which businesses and firms were compromised and infiltrated. Corruption became so bad that a report by Presidential advisor Petr Filippov issued in January 1994 estimated that 70-80% of private businesses and commercial banks were forced to pay protection money in order to survive. (Gustafson, p. 137, 1999)

In many ways, organized crime in Russia mirrored its North American counterparts, with money laundering, prostitution, and gambling being traditional areas of operation. Several high-profile figures came to prominence as Russian Mafia Dons. One of the most prominent was Otari KvantrishviliKvanstrishvili, who gained control over several industries in Moscow via his front company "Century 21". True to Mafia tradition, KvantrishviliKvanstrishvili also became very active in philanthropy, giving liberally to a variety of organizations, from schools, veterans groups, and sports teams. He became so influential that Yeltsin would even sign a decree in 1993 allowing one of his companies to import goods tax-free into the country. (Gustafson, p.145, 1999) Alarmingly, acts such as these would demonstrate the nexus of corruption, crime, and government in the new Russia that would become commonplace. With local vendors being required to have a permit from the cities or towns they lived in to do business and with local authorities being in league with organized crime, all the Mafia had to do was go to city hall to find out where a new business owner lived to find a new source in need of "protection". (Goldman, p.131, 1994) What would be considered criminal and unethical in the West was how business was done in Russia.

In foreign affairs, Yeltsin continued to seek a greater rapport with the West and the United States in particular. This effort paid off when Yeltsin was able to claim a major foreign policy triumph when on June 17, 1992, he and President Bush announced a major arms reduction deal that would drastically reduce their stockpiles of intercontinental ballistic missiles (ICBM) and multiple independently targetable reentry vehicles (multiple warheads on a single ICBM) to between 3,000 and 3,500 by the year 2003. While the United States would reduce submarine-launched missiles by half from 3,840 to 1,750, Russia's land-based missile force would be almost eliminated. Yeltsin's concessions were ultimately driven out of necessity in order to secure more aid from Washington. (Wines, June 17, 1992) This accord would come to be known as the START II (Strategic Arms Reduction Treaty), which would be signed by Bush and Yeltsin on

January 3, 1993, just weeks before the President left office. The accord, along with the joint Camp David statement in February, emphasizing that the Cold War was over, helped to further reinforce the public message that the United States and Russia, if not yet friends and allies, were no longer enemies intent on destroying one another (as well as the world). It was also reassuring to know that, regardless of how Yeltsin's economic and political reforms played out, the country's nuclear arsenal was secure and in the process of being dramatically reduced.

With the Russian economy in upheaval due to the sudden transition from a communist command model to a market-oriented one, Russia would be dependent on large amounts of foreign aid in order to keep the country running. Of particular importance in these matters was the International Monetary Fund (IMF), which gave billions in loans to Russia throughout the 1990s and beyond. For the time being, the West was on board with Yeltsin and willing to back him. However, this could easily change over time if Western leaders saw no progress in the economy or if Russia did not continue to liberalize politically via human and civil rights. President Yeltsin could not govern by decree indefinitely, and sooner or later, a new Constitution would have to be written to truly give the country lasting stability and democratic legitimacy. As events would show in October 1993, this last goal would result in violence and bloodshed as Yeltsin would finally dissolve the Supreme Soviet of Russia and the Congress of People's Deputies to obtain it.

As much upheaval and disorder as privatization caused throughout Russia in 1992, it would be a mistake to label all the reforms as failures. A declassified (as of 1999) CIA report on the subject, published in March 1993, gives us a comprehensive view of many of the changes that took place and their impact on the Russian economy. To start with, the economic turmoil faced by Russia had been well under way long before the demise of the Soviet Union and the centralized command economy. Since early 1990, industrial output for the country, measured at 100% from January 1989 figures, had slowly declined in fits and starts before plummeting from just over 90% capacity in early 1992 to just below 70% by late summer. The country's trade had also suffered greatly with old trading partners of the Soviet Union either not trading with the new Russian Federation or having to re-negotiate new trade deals. These trading relationships, along with the economic reforms, resulted in a substantial drop in both the country's exports and imports, with the former seeing a drop of around $15 billion (25% reduction) compared to 1991 levels and the latter around $10 billion (21% reduction). In concert with privatization, the credit and insurance industry had the highest-paid workers, with employees making over 40,000 rubles a month compared to the national average of 16,071 rubles for 1992.

However, the news was not all bad. Due to the ending of government subsidies and reductions in defense spending, the budget deficit was sharply reduced. Also, from housing, agriculture, and small business ownership, privatization had skyrocketed, although they fell far short of the government's goals. With Yeltsin and Gaidar's ending of price controls in January, food items and consumer goods returned to the shelves in grocery stores across most of the country. Still, most Russians had trouble being able to afford them due to out-of-control inflation. Many of the former republics also began to introduce their own currency that would either replace the ruble or be used concurrently with it until it was phased out of circulation completely, further complicating the economic situation. (CIA, economic survey, 1993) Despite all this, for now, the Russian people continued to back Yeltsin, his reforms, and his assurances that time was needed for them to be fully implemented and successful. Russia also was, nominally at least, a fully functioning government with elected representatives, civil and constitutional liberties, freedom of speech, assembly, and the press, which had begun during Glasnost. However, it is important to note that even though these freedoms were codified in the 1993 Russian Constitution, the strong power of the executive branch did not guarantee that these freedoms would be inalienable as would be the case when Yeltsin's successor came to power.

Despite Yeltsin's success in establishing new relationships with the West, conducting arms agreements and securing foreign aid, it was in the realm of foreign affairs where Russian disengagement would have the most disastrous consequences throughout the 90 s and beyond. Although the Soviets had withdrawn militarily from Afghanistan in early 1989, they had continued to support the Marxist and Russian-oriented government (People's Democratic Party of Afghanistan) of Mohammad Najibullah, who was in turn engaged in a power struggle with the same group of people the Russians had been fighting, the Mujahideen. During the Soviet invasion, it had been the Mujahideen who had led the resistance against Soviet forces and in the process received ample American aid and weaponry.

In September 1991, with the end of the Soviet Union rapidly approaching, U.S. Secretary of State James Baker and his Russian counterpart, Boris Pankin, agreed to halt all aid to their respective proxies that would become effective on January 1, 1992. Both the Mujahideen (backed by the U.S.) and the government of Najibullah (backed by the Soviet Union) were now left completely on their own. The CIA (Central Intelligence Agency) would no longer be able to operate legally in Afghanistan after over a decade on the ground, which would severely limit the U. S's ability to play any role in the political development of the country. Another consequence of disengagement would be the explosion of the drug trade as the year's poppy harvest resulted in massive quantities of heroin being shipped back into Russia and Europe via routes now controlled by the Russian Mafia. (Coll. p. 232-233. 2004) To place blame entirely on the Russians would be grossly unfair, as both the U.S. and the U.S.S.R. were seeking a way out of the Afghan sinkhole now that the Cold War was officially over. Public rhetoric aside, neither country truly believed that withdrawal and disengagement would bring about any sort of stability or peace between the rapidly splitting factions of the Mujahideen or the government of Najibullah, which grew weaker by the day.

With the sudden collapse of the Soviet Union in December 1991, aide and support for Najibullah's government completely evaporated and he was left on his own, resigning office in April 1992. Factions within factions fought against each other in a never-ending battle for control of a country that saw nothing but war for decades on end. The most prominent of these was the now infamous Taliban, which, after four years would gain power only to fight in yet another civil war, this time against a loose confederation called the Northern Alliance. The two groups would be at war from 1996 until December 2001, when with the backing of the United States the Taliban would be overthrown by the Northern Alliance. It was during the second civil war that the Taliban, an extremist Islamic government, offered sanctuary to the terrorist group Al-Qaeda who had just been expelled from Sudan.

From the sanctuary of Afghanistan and with the protection of the Taliban, Al-Qaeda under the leadership of Osama Bin-Laden, executed a series of terrorist attacks against the United States all throughout the 1990's culminating in the devastating attacks of September 11, 2001, in New York City killing almost 3,000 people. This would in turn trigger a U. S-led coalition which would bring another twenty-years of war to the country from 2001-2021. It is of the greatest irony that one of the most backwards, poverty-ridden and dangerous countries in the world ending up having a tremendous impact on the wealthiest most powerful one in the history of the planet. The world had largely ignored Afghanistan after the Soviet withdrawal in 1989 and the subsequent civil wars that followed. After the terrorist attacks on September 11, 2001, almost the entire first world would become involved in a twenty-year effort to defeat Al-Qaeda and the Taliban. First the Soviets and now just twelve-years later the U.S. and its allies would find out how difficult it was to not only win but to bring about any semblance of stability.

After the final U.S. withdrawal in August 2021, the Taliban easily took back power and promptly reinstated its harsh vision of an Islamic society based on Sharia Law. With the country being flooded with weapons from all over the world after four decades of war, it is safe to say that the Taliban can easily maintain control of Afghanistan for the foreseeable future. In early 1992, before he resigned from office, President Najibullah made a statement at a press conference that could just as easily apply to the present day as it did when he made it. He stated that, "We have a common task- Afghanistan, the U.S.A., and the civilized world- to launch a joint struggle against fundamentalism. If fundamentalism comes to Afghanistan, war will continue for many years. Afghanistan will turn into a center of world smuggling for narcotic drugs. Afghanistan will be turned into a center for terrorism." (Coll. p. 234-235. 2004) Whether history with respect to Afghanistan repeats itself, as it does so often, remains to be seen.

In some ways 1992, had been every bit a revolution for Russia as was the Bolshevik one of 1917. The country underwent seismic changes that impacted all aspects of society. The world's largest country (geographically at least) had attempted to change as rapidly as possible from a communist dictatorship to a multi-party representative democracy and from a centrally planned state-run economy to a free-market oriented one with private ownership. Historically speaking, change of this magnitude tends to cause massive disruptions on all levels of a society that even under the most favorable conditions takes time to come to fruition. To add to these difficulties was the historical fact that Russia itself had no recent history (or any history) of being a free society with all the institutions and norms inherent in it. Freedom of the press, separation of church and state and strong statues with regulatory bodies to enforce them were completely alien concepts.

Boris Yeltsin sincerely believed that with the right policies in place, Russia could, with some initial difficulty, be made into a free nation on par with the West. While the "shock therapy" reforms of Yegor Gaidar had brought about some success in jump-starting the efforts to privatize the economy, they had also caused astronomical inflation and a severe depreciation of the ruble. Throughout the 1990s, inflation and economic stability would remain serious issues. As international confidence in Russia's financial stability declined, the country would rely heavily on the IMF and its generous loan policies to secure aid time and again. In 1992 alone, the IMF would advance $959 million for Russia (IMF, 1992) and would give out $19.5 billion by the end of the decade, along with the World Bank giving $11.8 billion and the U.S. giving $5.45 billion. (Aslund, 2000)

In terms of bringing about real democratic governance to the country, it is safe to say that Yeltsin's record during his eight years in power were checkered at best. Even before the dissolution of the Soviet Union, Yeltsin had already been governing by simple decree. With these extraordinary powers, Yeltsin practically had the power to remake the country as he saw fit. As far reaching as these powers were, they eventually had to be renewed by the Supreme Soviet. Yeltsin's previously stated difficulties with Vice President Rutskoy and Chairman Khasbulatov had made this all but impossible.

After a national referendum on Yeltsin and his policies was held in April 1993 with a favorable result, Yeltsin attempted to call for early parliamentary elections on September 21 of that year as well as dissolving Parliament. Chairman Khasbulatov responded on September 23 by promptly declaring this action illegal, impeaching Yeltsin and then appointing Vice President Rutskoy as President of the Russian Federation. Yeltsin responded by shelling the White House and then storming it with Russian soldiers after a ten-day period of intense fighting in Moscow by pro and anti-Yeltsin forces. Out of the ashes of the October crisis, a new Russian Constitution was finally written. Gone were the Supreme Soviet of Russia and Congress of People's Deputies. Taking their place was the Federal Assembly which consisted of the Duma, the lower house and the Federation Council, the upper house. Yeltsin would now have total power over the appointment of the Prime Minister and could dissolve both houses of the assembly on a whim. This new Constitution gave the President of Russia almost absolute power by codifying the rule by decree system Yeltsin had already been using for over two-years. For a man who had been committed to multi-party democracy, the end of communism in Russia and stood on a tank to defy the leaders of the August 1991 coup, these actions smacked of outright authoritarianism. During the December elections of the new Federal Assembly, a sizable portion of the voters swept in candidates opposed to Yeltsin and his policies. Still, Yeltsin had secured a new government, a constitution to his liking and dispatched with Khasbulatov and Rutskoy and other anti-Yeltsin forces.

Russia would continue to struggle economically throughout the 1990's as well as face upheaval internally with both Chechen wars in the breakaway Republic of Chechnya from 1994 onwards. As Yeltsin ran for re-election in 1996, some feared that he might regress into total authoritarianism by canceling the election and declaring himself dictator.

Nevertheless, despite claims of media bias in favor of Yeltsin, he ran a surprisingly vigorous campaign and defeated Communist Party candidate Gennady Zyuganov 54.40% to 40.73% winning 40,203,948 votes to Zyuganov 30,102,288 (Aron. p. 629. 2000) in the second round of voting held on July 3, 1996. The election had been declared free and fair by several observers and third-party organizations and Zyuganov pledged to honor the results. For a man who had the ability to seize total power, certainly some credit is due for him choosing not to do so. For Russia, the first post-Cold War election had taken place and democracy, however nominally, had survived. Of course, it also must be noted that the support of Western leaders (and future aid) was also retained.

As Yeltsin's second term progressed, his health worsened as years of alcoholism and high stress began to take their toll. On August 9, 1999, Yeltsin appointed Vladimir Putin as his sixth Prime Minister (not counting himself at the beginning of his administration). Putin was a former KGB officer who had held a number of positions within Yeltsin's government. Yeltsin finally resigned as President on December 31, 1999, after eight-years in office and months before his term expired. Putin's very first decree as acting President was to prohibit any prosecution of Yeltsin or his family who had been scandal ridden towards the end of his presidency. It was no secret that Putin had lamented the break-up of the Soviet Union and was less than fully committed to the ideals of democracy and a free society.

As he consolidated his power, his regime became more authoritarian with the familiar totalitarian trope of jailed opponents and less freedom in the media. Putin continued to prosecute Yeltsin's war in Chechnya as well as start new ones against Georgia in 2008 and Ukraine in 2014 followed by a full-scale invasion in February 2022 that continues to the present day. Having served a full two terms as President from 2000-2008 and being constitutionally prohibited from serving a third consecutive one, Putin then served a symbolic term as Prime Minister from 2008-2012 before returning to the presidency in 2012. During his successor Dmitry Medvedev's term as President, the terms of office were extended to six-years and Putin was re-elected in 2018 and 2024 in elections that have widely been viewed as fraudulent. In early 2020, an executive order was issued by Putin that allowed him to serve two more six-year terms. A law to this effect was passed by the Federal Assembly after a sham referendum was held from June 25-July 1, 2020. This means that Putin could potentially stay in office as President of Russia until 2036.

In light of Putin's twenty-five-year rule as either President or Prime Minister, it would be easy to conclude that the hopes and dreams of democracy that seemed so strong in early 1992 were, along with Communism itself, consigned to the ash bin of history. Although it is true that freedom of the press is non-existent in Russia, its current government hopelessly corrupt and its elections all but rigged and fraudulent, there is still a strong spirit of resistance to Putin and his regime. Dissidents speak out against the war in Ukraine and countless journalists have risked their very lives to criticize Putin. While these efforts have little hope of success in changing the current character of the Russian government, they resoundingly show that many Russians retain the ideals of fairness and freedom and are also not afraid to stand up and speak out despite the potentially deadly consequences.

Boris Yeltsin was sincere in his desire to bring about a multi-party democracy and radically change the Russian economy into a capitalistic oriented one with private ownership. He knew all too well during the period of 1989-1991 that the Soviet Union and Communism's days were numbered and that change was inevitable. In this he differed greatly from Mikhail Gorbachev who whole-heartily believed that Socialism and the

Communist ideal could be reformed and preserved for the future. Having been disgraced at the hands of Gorbachev in November 1987 and not being totally exiled or even executed was proof in and of itself that times were changing. However, like Gorbachev, Yeltsin's arrogance and desire for an all-powerful presidency and the ensuing October 1993 coup undermined his claim to be a genuine democrat.

Yet in fairness it must be noted that Yeltsin faced an unprecedented challenge in trying to accomplish what he sought and that the headwinds that he faced both politically and historically were simply too strong to prevail against. This more than likely would have been the case for any Russian leader after the Cold War and beyond. In that first year of 1992 that Russians and the Republics lived free of Communism, a great experiment was conducted to see if Russia could become something it never had been before, a free society. That hope still has yet to be realized and it is doubtful that it can while Putin remains in office but the yearning is still there among the Russian people. In order to fully understand the significance of Russia's attempt to become free, it is necessary for one to also have an understanding of the events leading up to 1992 and what has come afterwards as those forces are still playing out to this day. Vladimir Putin will not be in power forever and it is difficult to know what course Russia will take when that day comes.

Yeltsin's most tangible accomplishment in 1992 would be his foresight to seek a new relationship with the West and to safely transport, disarm and destroy large amounts of the former Soviet Union's nuclear arsenal. The final days of the Soviet Union and the first few ones of the Russian Federation was also a very dangerous period where any number of variables could have resulted in disaster or a nuclear exchange. The fact that despite all the turmoil surrounding these events that it did not is in and of itself a worthy accomplishment. After all, we are still alive. For now.

1992

Throughout 1992, Russian citizens had to deal with a shortage of goods and hyperinflation brought on by Yeltsin's reforms.

Gorbachev and Yeltsin's relationship was one of contention before the final collapse of the U.S.S.R.

The old hammer and sickle of the Soviet Union was replaced by the new Russian tricolor in the Kremlin on December 25, 1991.

Yegor Gaidar: The architect of Yeltsin's crash privatization of the Russian economy, known as 'shock therapy'.

As 1992 began, President Yeltsin made a major effort to cultivate strong relationships with the West, particularly with U.S President George H.W. Bush. It was largely successful as he would help secure arms control agreements and, of course, foreign aid.

CHAPTER 2

3's A Party: The 1992 Presidential Campaign

The most memorable moment of 1992 for a majority of Americans would likely be the U.S. presidential election. The man that emerged the winner is almost just as remarkable as the circumstances in which he was elected. For the past twelve years the country had been under the rule of two Republican Presidents. Both of whom are among the oldest men to ever hold the office. Faster than most people could realize, the Cold War which had divided the world into two armed camps for almost half a century was over. With the collapse of the Soviet Union, the entire order of the past 50 years (political, cultural and social) also collapsed as well. With the menace of the Soviet Union and Communism suddenly gone, it became possible the ascension to the Presidency of a man whom a mere four years ago would have been all but impossible. The election itself was a once in a life-time affair with a sitting President who only less than two years ago stood triumphant with the most decisive American military victory since the end of WWII and an approval rating of over 90%. Now just one year later, amid the U.S. economy mired in recession, President George H.W. Bush saw his approval ratings plummet as well as a challenge from his conservative base in Patrick Buchannan. Buchannan, as it turned out, was just the beginning of Bush's problems. Having survived the Buchanan's primary challenge, Bush would then face Independent candidate and Billionaire Ross H. Perot in the general election as well as Governor Bill Clinton of Arkansas. The entire campaign was itself a rollercoaster ride from start to finish with wild accusations thrown about and enough scandals for a soap opera etc. Although future elections would involve more money, more polling and certainly more emotional issues, never before and never since has the country experienced such a bizarre and unique election.

George H.W. Bush was probably (as one of his 1988 campaign commercials suggested) the best qualified person to ever become president. A man born into privilege and the son of a wealthy Wall Street banker, George Bush had never had to worry about money or anything material. Born on June 12, 1924, in Milton, Massachusetts he grew up in a prominent New England family. As a child, he was educated at the elite east coast Prep School Philip's Academy in Andover, MA. Bush chose to enlist in the Navy upon graduation in 1942, becoming the youngest U.S. Navy pilot in World War II serving with distinction and being shot down while flying a bombing mission over Chi Chi Jima in 1944. After the war ended in 1945, Bush returned to the states where he married Barbra Rye of New York. He then enrolled in Yale University where he took a heavy course load and was captain of the baseball team. After he graduated, Bush had the choice of several plum Wall Street jobs which he turned down to move to Texas in an attempt to strike it big in the booming oil business.

Bush made a fortune in the oil business and eventually was bitten by the same political bug that had struck his father (Prescott Bush, a US senator from Connecticut) and became involved in local Texas politics in the early 1960's. Bush's first run for office was in 1964 for a U.S. Senate seat in Texas, a race which he lost badly to the incumbent Ralph Yarbrough in a year that proved to be a landslide one for the Democrats in the wake of the Kennedy assassination. Bush then ran for a congressional seat two years later and won handily. During his time in office Bush showed that he was not afraid to put his principles in action even if they might cost him politically (a trait that would arguably cost him his re-election as president) when in 1968 he voted with President Lyndon Johnson to outlaw discrimination in public housing, a move deeply unpopular in his district. After four years in Congress, Bush made another run for a U.S. Senate seat in Texas in 1970. Despite help from the Nixon White House, Bush lost again. This time it was to Lloyd Bensten, a former congressman who had defeated incumbent Sen. Ralph Yarbourgh in the primary earlier that year. Bush went on to serve in a variety of administrative posts in the Nixon and Ford Administrations from 1971-1977 which included U.N. Ambassador, Chairman of the Republican Party, Liaison to China and Director of Central Intelligence (C.I.A.) respectively. After a 2nd place finish in the 1980 Republican Presidential Primaries, he was offered the Vice Presidential slot at the last moment by Ronald Reagan. After eight years as Vice President, Bush won the Presidency in 1988 in a landslide victory against Massachusetts Governor Michael S. Dukakis. Bush's presidency was beset by seismic international changes. In November 1989, the hated Berlin Wall which divided East and West Germany was finally torn down and Germany reunified less than a year later. The Soviet Union Collapsed on December 25, 1991 and overnight the Cold War of 45 years ended. Not with a bang, but with a whimper. Bush had also presided over the lightning quick Gulf War which saw the United States win the most overwhelming victory with minimal casualties since WWII. In the aftermath of the war, his approval rating skyrocketed to 91% and it was thought that his re-election was an inevitability. Then the economy slowed down dramatically, and the country entered a recession. This was due partly to the end of the Cold War and the subsequent reduction in military spending. Bush also had to contend with a more rightward leaning Republican Congress on issues of spending and taxes which will be discussed shortly. All of a sudden Bush was facing challenges from three directions including his own party.

In order to fully understand the magnitude of Bush's defeat we must have a comprehensive look at the events surrounding his issues with the Republican base and the man who stepped forward to challenge him. Patrick Joseph Buchanan was born on November 2, 1938, in Washington D.C. to a large upper middle class Catholic family. Attending then graduating from Georgetown and Columbia (1960 & 1962) Buchanan then entered a career in journalism. His first job out of college was for the St. Louis Globe-Democrat. After four years of working for the newspaper, he was hired by Richard Nixon as an opposition researcher during his campaigns on behalf of Republicans in the midterm elections of 1966 and then his successful run for the presidency in 1968. During this time, he became known for his hard hitting and highly partisan speeches that appealed to the traditional working class. Once Nixon became President, it was Buchanan that coined the phrase "Silent Majority" which was used to great effect by the president. After Nixon's resignation in August 1974, Buchanan returned to writing and appearing on a number of political talk shows over the next eleven years such as syndicated The McLaughlin Group and CNN'S Crossfire. Shortly after Ronald Reagan's landslide re-election in 1984, Buchanan was hired as the Reagan White House Communications Director in February 1985. He served in this capacity for just over two years until his departure in March 1987.

On January 20, 1989, George H.W. Bush was inaugurated as President and Ronald Reagan left office. Having won the White House with the support of the religious right and Reagan Republicans, it was assumed that Bush would carry on the conservative legacy of Reagan's eight years in office. However, as events unfolded it became clear that Bush was a more centrist Republican wary of rightwing ideologues and evangelicals. For most of the Reagan conservatives the final straw came during the budget negotiations in the fall of 1990 when in order to reduce the growing federal and national deficit, Bush had to publicly go back on his 1988 pledge of "Read My Lips, No New Taxes!!" and agree to increases on several different kinds of taxes in order to obtain spending cuts from the Democratic Congress (Omnibus Budget Reconciliation Act of 1990). In retrospect it was a necessary and responsible course of action in order to address the national deficit which had grown to over $3 trillion in the previous decade. Not so for the Conservatives and Pat Buchanan. In their eyes it was a betrayal of the conservative principles of not increasing taxes at all costs. For Bush they felt it was political suicide and in the end they were right. The point of no return had been reached from the right and their patience and trust in Bush was completely gone.

On December 10, 1991, Buchanan formally announced his intention to challenge President Bush in the upcoming Republican primaries. The speech was fraught with ringing declarations against Bush, Liberals, internationalism, etc. Buchanan stated that he would pass on Western Heritage for future generations and not allow it to be "dumped onto some landfill called multiculturalism". He promised to defend the Judeo-Christian values and stated that man had "forgotten God". In addressing the social ills of society from gang violence, drug abuse and the A.I.D.S. epidemic, he stated that society was suffering from "a chronic moral sickness." In attacking President Bush's leadership, Buchanan stated that it was not Congress who had cut, "a seedy backroom deal with the big spenders on Capitol Hill". His style could be described as coarse, blunt, confrontational, or even incendiary. Buchanan declared that his campaign was open to voters of "both parties and of no party." (Kornacki, 2018, p. 153: all quotes) He lambasted Congress and the ruling class for being "ossified and out of touch." The speech lasted only around 15 minutes, but it had its intended effect. Irrespective of Buchanan's chances of winning the nomination, there could be no doubt that his message had great appeal among the far right and others as well.

The New Hampshire Republican Primary was held on February 18, 1992. When the polls closed, it became clear that Buchanan and his supporters had delivered a huge shock to the Republican Party. Out of all the ballots cast, Bush had won 92,271 (53.2%) to Buchanan's 65,106 (37.5%). (Wikipedia.org) The fact that Bush emerged victorious was irrelevant. That Buchanan had managed to garner such a high percentage was treated as a victory. Never before had a sitting President had such a stiff challenge, let alone from someone who was a mere commentator and journalist. As Buchanan himself had said throughout the campaign, "Buchanan Brigades will meet King George's hollow army head on and cut through it like butter!" Although Buchanan would not win any primaries, nor would he ever match his New Hampshire showing, he would stay in the race all through the primary season. On March 7 in the South Carolina primary, he managed to win 25.7% to Bush's 66.9%, and on June 2 (the last day of the primaries) he polled a noticeable 26.4% to Bush's 74.6% in California. In over four months of campaigning in the primaries, Buchanan had won 2,899,488 votes for 23% of the vote. (Wikipedia.org) He had proved beyond all doubt that he spoke for a significant portion of the Republican electorate and was a force that had to be reckoned with. Still, Bush had won re-nomination, and now it appeared that there was nothing more for Buchanan to do but fall in line, endorse Bush, and go back into the woodwork. Or so it seemed.

At the conclusion of the primary season, Buchanan endorsed Bush after being courted by his campaign. In return Buchanan was to be given a prime time speaking slot at the Republican National Convention which was being held in Houston, TX in mid-August. On August 17, 1992, Buchanan's turn came to speak at the convention. Although the Bush people had an advance copy of the speech they were more concerned with Buchanan's support for Bush than they were with its actual content. As he began to speak it should have been obvious that the speech was classic Buchanan. Which was not good news for the Bush campaign.

In what would come to be known as the "Culture War" speech, Buchanan reprised many of the themes he had mentioned in his announcement speech eight months earlier, as well as new material. He spoke of the Democratic Convention as the "greatest single exhibition of cross-dressing in American political history" and criticized Clinton's lack of foreign policy experience as having "been confined to having breakfast once at the International House of Pancakes." He also warned that Clinton and Clinton would herald, "abortion on demand, a litmus test for the Supreme Court, homosexual rights, discrimination against religious schools, women in combat units." There was also plenty of mockery for Vice Presidential nominee Al Gore, whom he referred to as "Prince Albert." Yet he also firmly praised President Bush and his accomplishments, particularly in foreign policy, and claimed Republicans won the Cold War. He railed against Clinton's character while contrasting it favorably with Bush's, stating that Bush had volunteered for WWII while Clinton, "sat up in a dormitory room in Oxford, England and figured out how to dodge the draft." He then followed this up by asking the delegates between Bush and Clinton who had the moral authority to send young men into battle. Buchanan also gave a full-throated defense of the Reagan years and rebuked those who would say it had been a dark time in America's history. The audience roared its approval, and Buchanan was interrupted several times with cries of "Go Pat Go!!"(Kornacki, 2018, p. 194-195: all quotes) While the speech had accomplished its immediate goal of uniting the party and "coming home" to Bush, it had also put on display what many perceived to be the harsh, divisive rhetoric Bush's handlers had been hoping to avoid, as it turned off moderates, independents, and came across as exclusionary. The die had been cast. While Buchanan's culture war speech did not alone change the nature of American politics and the Republican Party, it crystallized these sentiments into everyday political rhetoric that would become commonplace on the Right as the 1990s progressed. The fear of being "primaried" in future elections for being insufficiently conservative was one Republican politicians would always have to consider when casting their votes on various issues going forward. The themes and tone of the "Culture War" speech would go on to play an important role in American politics and future elections that endures to this very day.

The winters of New Hampshire are incredibly harsh and for one Democratic candidate for President this was especially the case in January 1992. Arkansas Governor Bill Clinton had just made his promise that if his supporters stuck with him, he would be with them, "until the last dog dies". The first of what would later become known as the "Bimbo Eruptions" had just occurred (at least the first one that the whole nation became aware of). Gennifer Flowers, a state employee in Arkansas, had just come forward and claimed that she had an affair with Clinton. It looked as if Clinton seemed doomed to repeat the fate of 1988 presidential candidate Gary Hart who had been forced to withdraw from the race after it was revealed that he had an affair with a woman on a boat called "monkey business". However, the country was about to learn why Bill Clinton was called the "Comeback Kid", due to an uncanny ability to recover from any crises whether it be personal or political and survive. Just 3 months before in Little Rock Arkansas, Bill Clinton had launched his lifelong ambition of becoming President of the United States, a dream he had held since his teenage years.

Born on August 19, 1946, in Hope, Arkansas to a recently widowed Virginia Cassidy, it was obvious from the beginning that young Clinton was highly intelligent. At an early age, he had acquired a passion for politics which he later would perfect into a career. He was unquestionably intelligent, articulate and knew policy inside and out and at just age thirty-two he would become the nation's youngest Governor of Arkansas in 1979. The English philosopher Francis Bacon once said, "All rising to a great place is by winding stair" this saying seemed especially true of Bill Clinton's life. After just one term as Governor of Arkansas he was voted out of office and suffered a nervous breakdown in 1980. Yet just two years later he won back the governorship and won re-election three more times. In the mid-1980's Clinton became chair of the Democratic Leadership Council (DLC) an organization designed to help move the Democratic party back to the center politically after the disastrous defeats of 1980 and 1984.

Al From, the creator of the DLC, very aptly realized that no one could communicate and sell the Democratic party's ideals better than Bill Clinton. Clinton's journey to national political stardom was not always smooth sailing. At the 1988 Democratic Convention in Atlanta, GA nominating Massachusetts Governor Michael Dukakis for President, Clinton gave a badly received speech in which he talked for too long and after a while the delegates stopped paying attention. In 1989, his marriage almost fell apart over his many affairs with other women. Nevertheless, Clinton had built a solid resume as a centrist Democrat that could take the party, and himself above all else, back into the White House. As

Clinton struggled and fought through the nominating process of 1992 it was clear that a change was under way. By June of 1992, Clinton had captured enough delegates to win the Democratic nomination despite an all-out effort by former California Governor Jerry Brown. As was obvious for all to see, Clinton was young, listened to rock and roll and even appeared on the Arsenio Hall talk show. He could become the first baby boom president, but he had to get elected first.

Governor Clinton would have two strong personal assets to help him weather the storms of the campaign. The first was his wife, one Hillary Rodham Clinton. It goes without saying that Mrs. Clinton was a force in her own right long before she had met and married Bill Clinton. Born on October 27, 1947, in Chicago, Illinois, young Hillary excelled academically and graduated from the all-women's Wellesley College. She then went on to Yale Law School, where she met Bill Clinton, who was also a student in the program. Upon graduation, she married Bill and moved with him back to Arkansas, working at the prestigious Rose Law Firm while he briefly taught at the University of Arkansas and then began his political career. She would be a steadying force for her husband as he served as Governor of Arkansas and took an active role in the affairs of state government. Knowing that her husband would end up in the arena of presidential politics, she was not one to wilt under pressure or sit in the background. After Gennifer Flowers went public with her claims of having an affair with Bill Clinton for twelve years, it was Hillary who came to his defense. In a January 26, 1992, joint interview on the CBS TV Show 60 Minutes, Hillary projected a defiant and confident demeanor as she defended her husband's character and their marriage a few weeks prior to the pivotal New Hampshire primary. She made a pointed reference to country singer Tammy Wynette's "Stand By Your Man" when explaining that she wasn't standing by Clinton out of marital obligation but because of love and belief in him. It worked. Clinton would recover from the Flowers episode and go on to win a surprising second place in the New Hampshire Primary, garnering 41,542 votes for 24.78% of the vote against former Massachusetts Senator Paul Tsongas, 55,666 and 33.21%. (Wikipedia.org) Not since Eleanor Roosevelt had Americans seen such an outspoken and independent spouse in a campaign. Yet Mrs. Roosevelt did not live in the era of television, nor did she have to deal with allegations of her husband's infidelity (at least not publicly). Either way, it certainly was a first for American Politics.

No Presidential Campaign is ever complete without the colorful Political Strategist/ Advisor who helps his or her candidate throughout the storms of modern campaigning. George H.W. Bush had Lee Atwater, George W. had Karl Rove and Barack Obama had David Axelrod. For Bill Clinton in 1992 this man was Chester James Carville Jr. also known as the "Ragin Cajun". Born October 25, 1944, Carville grew up in a large family in a town that he was ironically named after. After flunking out of Louisiana State University (LSU), Carville did a brief stint in the U.S. Marines before returning to LSU and completing his undergraduate degree and then going on to law school and earning his J.D. After he finished law school Carville took to mainly practice law and briefly teaching Middle School Science. By the beginning of the 1980's Carville had begun to gravitate towards politics and joined Weill-Strother, a political consulting firm.

Carville worked on many campaigns throughout the 1980's but his big break came in 1991 when he managed the Pennsylvania U.S. Senate campaign of Harris Wofford in a special election that November. Despite trailing his opponent by a wide margin initially (former U.S. Attorney General and Governor Dick Thornburgh), with the guidance of Carville, Wofford was able to mount an amazing comeback and win the election by over 300,000 votes for a winning percentage of 55% to Thornburgh's 44% in the November special election. (Wikipedia.org) Just one month later, Carville would be hired on by Governor Clinton as his campaign manager for his presidential bid. Carville's personality and heavy southern accent added a lot of flavor to the Clinton campaign. Yet the "Ragin Cajun" pioneered a strategy that took no prisoners and was the pinnacle of hardball campaigning. Fully aware that Dukakis's failure to respond effectively against Bush's attacks in 1988 had destroyed his image and chances of winning, Carville insisted that every attack made by Bush and later Perot would be immediately answered and rebutted. It was Carville, along with his associate and fellow strategist Paul Begala, as well as George Stephanopoulos, who set up what would become known as the "war room," where strategy would be plotted and responses to scandals, accusations and any other "incoming" as he phrased it would be dealt with. It was Carville who labeled the Gennifer Flowers story as "cash for trash" and defended Clinton's character time and again. Finally, it was Carville who laid out the messaging of the campaign in 3 points. 1. "It's the economy, stupid" 2. "Change vs. more of the same" and 3. "Don't forget healthcare." Carville certainly had his work cut out for him. As Carville and everyone around Clinton quickly learned, it was one crisis after another. Along with the womanizing, trust, and character issues, there came the potentially fatal problem of how Clinton had handled the draft in 1969 at the height of the Vietnam War.

After graduating from Georgetown University in 1968, Clinton was awarded a prestigious Rhodes Scholarship to study at Oxford University in England. While at Oxford, Clinton was granted a draft deferment as was typical of most students at the time. Yet Clinton had ambitions of attending Law School in the near future and knew that his deferments would more than likely end upon leaving Oxford. Clinton sought to avoid being drafted by joining an R.O.T.C program at the University of Arkansas. After signing a letter of intent that he would join the program while attending law school, Clinton decided to remain at Oxford and not join the R.O.T.C. program. To justify his decision, he wrote a lengthy and articulate letter to the U.S. Army Colonel, Eugene Holmes, who had been assisting him in getting into the program which was released by the Pentagon in February 1992 just as voting began in the primaries. The letter shows a young Clinton full of anguish over his decision and the events surrounding him. Clinton admitted that he had reneged on a promise to join the R.O.T.C. program but had then subsequently registered for the draft and was not called up. Still, the implication when the issue arose was that Clinton had avoided the draft (or dodged it) by less than honest methods. For a man wishing to become Commander in Chief and have the power to send young men and women into battle, it was an issue that touched on a lot of nerves, particularly among veterans. While many in the campaign feared the issue could be fatal to Clinton, Carville took an opposite view. In keeping with his campaign philosophy of rapid response, he argued that the full letter should be made public as it showcased Clinton's intelligence and him articulating his genuine belief that the war was wrong while still loving his country deeply. Although the draft issue would not entirely go away, thanks to Carville's strategy it was somewhat neutralized.

Bill Clinton was very lucky to have the likes of James Carville, Paul Begala, George Stephanopoulos, and his spouse, Hillary Clinton, on his team. As formidable as Bill Clinton the campaigner was, it stands to reason he may not have prevailed without their expertise and advice. The campaign was a well-oiled machine, seemingly capable of withstanding any crises that would have sunk any other major candidate. Its smooth operation was in stark contrast to the Bush campaign, which never recovered from the untimely death of the President's strategist, Lee Atwater, who passed away in March 1991 from brain cancer. Indeed, Atwater had been quoted in reference to the 1992 election that, "I ain't worried about Mario Cuomo, Bill Clinton does worry me." (Hamilton. 2003. p. 539) Bush instead had to take the dramatic step of bringing his distinguished Secretary of State James A. Baker to run his re-election effort just two months prior to the election. Bush did have some capable hands on deck, most notably one Mary Matalin, who ironically started dating Carville during the campaign. Like Carville, Matalin had worked in political campaigns for quite some time, most notably during then-Vice President Bush's successful White House bid in 1988. As Deputy Campaign Manager, she showed unwavering loyalty to Bush throughout the re-election effort. Still, it could be said that with all the factors working against Bush from the economy and the recession, the obstacles were just too much for any incumbent political campaign team to overcome.

However dynamic and exciting the Clinton candidacy was, it was, for a time in the summer of 1992, dwarfed by another equally interesting and no less colorful candidate, Ross H. Perot. In the unique and once in a lifetime circumstance of the 1992 election Ross Perot came onto the scene as the independent candidate who would save the nation from the ballooning federal budget deficit, revive the economy and torpedo free trade so there would be no "giant sucking sound" going south. He financed his campaign largely with his own money and was able to garner enough support in the public opinion polls that, despite dropping out of the race once before, he was allowed to participate in the presidential debates once he re-entered the contest. Although no one can deny the potency or force of Perot's candidacy, what made him so special was not so much the fact that he was in the race but the possibility that he might actually win. Never before had a third-party candidate performed so well, inspired by such an ardent following, and for a time seemed credible.

Ross Perot's claim to outsider status was as genuine as they get. Despite his enormous amount of wealth, Perot had never been elected to or held a public office. Perot was born on June 27, 1930, and was a graduate of the U.S. Naval Academy, where he helped to write the honor code. After leaving the Navy in 1957, he began his business career as a salesman for IBM in the late 1950s when computers were merely in their infancy. He very quickly established a reputation for doggedness and tenacity that served him well all throughout his career. A signature trait of Perot was to always ask for the hardest assignments the company could give so he could make the most money. Perot would always outwork all co-workers in the never-ending chase for the dollar. As he bluntly put it, "Look, the only thing I'm doing different from the other salesmen is that I work all day and they don't." (Posner. 1996. p. 27) Perot founded EDS (Electronic Data Systems), a computer company that specialized in medical records keeping, and then boomed shortly after the creation of Medicare and Medicaid in 1965. Perot's first major brush with the limelight came in late 1969 when he dreamt up the idea to deliver plane loads of medical supplies, food, blankets, and other comforts to American POWs in North Vietnam. Although the attempt failed due to North Vietnam's refusal of Perot's two plane loads of supplies to land, it did succeed in making him a household name and highlighting the cause of American POWs. It was also during the POW episode that an important aspect of Perot's personality came out. Perot's effort had been given backing by the Nixon White House, although they did not expect him to succeed in delivering the supplies.

After being refused permission to land by the North Vietnamese, Perot began to fly around to various locations to try and find another route of approach that the North Vietnamese would find acceptable, even going so far as to repackage the supplies to meet new demands the North Vietnamese placed on package dimensions. Perot's independent streak greatly annoyed the Nixon White House. Several high-ranking officials went so far as to attempt to block Perot's plane's clearance to take off from Vientiane, Laos. (Posner, 1996. p. 61-64) A former EDS employee stated bluntly that, "Ross sets his own rules. He's not very good at any position but coach." (Posner. 1996. p. 63) Perot's loose cannon approach was repeated when, in late 1978, two EDS employees were arrested in Tehran, Iran, on the eve of the Iranian Revolution. Perot recruited a small squad of employees who were Vietnam Veterans, along with a Special Forces Colonel who had led an unsuccessful attempt to rescue U.S. POWS from North Vietnam, with combat experience, to rescue the imprisoned employees. Perot even visited Iran and lobbied aggressively for their release. At one point, Perot avoided arrest only due to the intervention of the U.S. embassy in Tehran. Once the two employees were moved to a more secure location, the operation to rescue them fell apart.

The 1980s would turn out to be a very good decade for Perot. In 1984, EDS was bought out by General Motors, and Perot received over $930 million in a very smart business move. (Posner. 1996. p. 183) The American public would soon become very familiar with Perot's unique personal style. The POW issue championed by Perot during the war began to fester throughout the 1980's with Perot making public statements that he unequivocally believed that American servicemen were still being held prisoner in Vietnam long after the war had ended. Perot's statements and belief that the US government knew about the POWs being held severely strained his relationship with the Reagan/ Bush White House.

What makes the 1992 presidential election so extraordinary, is that less than 2 years prior to its occurrence, it was thought that the election would be no contest. Incumbent President George H.W. Bush had been viewed as invincible in the wake of the swift victory of the Gulf War in early 1991. His approval ratings stood at over 91% and no Democrat had won the White House since Jimmy Carter was elected in 1976 almost 16 years ago. Compounding all these difficulties for any Democratic challenger was the party's perceived weakness on issues of national security. Since Richard Nixon was elected in 1968, national security and foreign affairs had been viewed as the exclusive domain of the Republican Party. After all, the collapse of the Soviet Union and the end of the Cold War were victories claimed by Republicans.

Declaring his candidacy in October 1991, Arkansas Governor Bill Clinton was given virtually no chance to win the nomination much less the general election. However, after surviving a grueling primary campaign along with the aforementioned "bimbo eruptions", Gov. Clinton secured the Democratic nomination in June of 1992 winning all contests held on that day and finally forcing Jerry Brown to drop out of the race. The womanizing, draft evasion and character issues that had dogged him in the primary had taken a toll on his favorability ratings and he needed to find a way to reposition himself with the political center. At the Democratic National Convention held in New York City in July of 1992, he chose Tennessee Senator Al Gore as his running mate to help give him some leverage in foreign affairs. The choice was well received but surprised many pundits. Nevertheless, the Clinton/Gore ticket soared to a 25% lead in the polls following the convention. (Kornacki, 2018, p. 192)

Traditionally most presidential candidates will choose a running mate from a different regional area or with less/more moderate views than the candidate themselves to give the ticket some more balance. Recent examples of this include conservative Ronald Reagan choosing moderate

George Bush and then moderate George Bush choosing conservative Dan Quayle. New Democrat Bill Clinton from Arkansas chose new Democrat Al Gore from neighboring Tennessee. President Bush stuck with current Vice President Dan Qualye who was viewed as a liability more than anything else. The Vice President had always suffered from a public perception of being lightweight and not very intelligent. A perception that was no doubt not helped when he recommended a student add an E at the end of potato at a spelling bee contest he attended in June 1992. Throughout the summer before the convention, there had even been talk of dropping Quayle from the ticket and recruiting Colin Powell to take his place on the ticket. It was hoped that the well regarded and highly popular first black Chairman of the Joint Chiefs during the Gulf War and the first black National Security Advisor during the last year of the Reagan administration might provide some much-needed lift to the ticket.

The Republican National Convention was beset by harsh and divisive rhetoric that alienated moderate voters and left a bad taste in the public's mouth. This was topped off by an over-the-top exclusionary speech by Patrick Buchannan condemning anything that was not sufficiently conservative in America. A speech made by Second Lady Marilyn Qualye renouncing feminism and claiming that most women were happy to be mothers and stay at home came across as especially backwards and out of touch. One bright spot was a speech by A.I.D.S activist Mary Fischer, who was also H.I.V positive, that encouraged research to cure the disease as well as compassion and help for those that were suffering from it. Her statement that, "A.I.D.S. doesn't care if you are Republican or Democrat, gay or straight" particularly struck a chord. President Bush gave an acceptance speech that had little to offer policy wise in terms of relieving the deep recession the country had been experiencing. To make matters worse, the anti-tax conservative base that had been so crucial in helping the Republicans win the past three elections, had all but deserted Bush in the wake of his 1990 budget deal with congressional Democrats to raise taxes in return for spending caps to control the budget deficit and in the process breaking his all too well known no new tax pledge from the 1988 convention. Bush was also having problems with the Reagan wing of the party who were disappointed in his lack of rapport with conservative activists. The culmination of this disappointment was led by the candidacy of Patrick Buchannan.

As if Bush was not having enough trouble with the economy and other domestic issues, his party and the Democrats, he was about to be attacked from another direction, dimming his re-election prospects even further. For years Ross Perot held a grudge against George H.W. Bush over several matters. First had been Bush's refusal to join him in a business venture in the 1970's. The second had been in the late 1980's when he alleged that US POWs were still being held in Southeast Asia and engaged in secret talks with Vietnamese officials which further damaged relations with the Reagan administration. Perot appeared on *Larry King Live* in February 1992 and announced his intention to run for President as an Independent if his supporters would be able to get his name on the ballot in all 50 states. Throughout the spring and summer, Perot's support continued to gain momentum and at one point he was even in the polls with the two major party candidates. Even more telling was a march by thousands of supporters in Austin, TX on May 11, 1992, to the State House heeding his call to place his

name on the ballot. In order to be placed on the ballot in Texas, Perot needed 54,000 signatures on a petition from Texas residents. His supporters came armed with 225,000. (Kornacki, 2018, p. 167) This was more than four times the amount necessary. The demonstration was so large that a nervous George W. Bush, who was working on his father's re-election campaign, watching from an office window immediately sounded the alarm with the President imploring him not to dismiss Perot. In some aspects it was advice that was never truly heeded. This drama played out in many states over the coming weeks as Perot surged in the polls.

Despite his momentum, in some areas Perot clearly struggled. When Perot appeared at an NAACP convention in mid-July, he caused great consternation by referring to the predominantly Black audience as "You People" and "Your People" when discussing issues impacting the Black Community. Such blatant insensitivity did not serve Perot well among potential minority voters. As stated previously, Perot liked to have total control over his endeavors be it business, politics or anything for that matter and as a result he seemed to have trouble taking advice from anyone. Perot had taken on high profile figures from both parties such as Hamilton Jordan who had served as Jimmy Carter's Chief of Staff and Ed Rollins who had run Ronald Regan's 1984 landslide re-election campaign. Both would have great difficulty working with Perot and Rollins would end up quitting after Perot fired one of his colleagues. Between the internal friction within his own camp as well as his claim that the Bush campaign was attempting to wreck his daughter's wedding with fake photos, his standing with voters suffered considerably and by the end of July he had withdrawn from the race altogether.

With the end of the conventions and the withdrawal of Perot, only Clinton and Bush faced each other for the time being. By the end of September when the debates normally occurred, Clinton continued to hold a decisive lead over Bush. On October 1, 1992, Perot suddenly re-entered the race and asked to be included in the debates due to his high polling numbers. Both the Bush and Clinton campaigns consented to Perot's inclusion, and he was allowed to participate believing that his presence would help them as well as undermine him. How wrong they were. On October 11, 1992, the first ever three-way presidential debate was held at Washington University in St. Louis, Missouri. From his opening remarks onward Perot displayed a strong grasp of the issues, a folksy and plain sense of humor such as looking under the hood and figuring out what the problem was with the economy, and the ability to deliver many a zinger. When asked about his lack of experience, Perot conceded that his opponents had a point and that he had no experience in, "running up a four trillion-dollar debt."

The most heated exchanges came when Bush attacked Clinton for his participation in Vietnam War protests while he was a Rhodes Scholar at Oxford University. Clinton's alleged character issue was the main line of attack that the Bush campaign had been using against the Governor (considering the deepening recession and Bush's lack of ideas to combat it, the only one available). Bush stated that his issue was not with Clinton's patriotism but his judgment and that choosing to protest the war in a foreign country reflected poorly on the judgment of someone, especially if they want to be commander in chief. Clinton sensing his opportunity to attack the issue that had plagued him since the primaries, turned directly to President Bush and said, "When Joe McCarthy went around this country attacking people's patriotism, he was wrong ... and a Senator from Connecticut stood up to him, named Prescott Bush. Your father was right to stand up to Joe McCarthy. You were wrong to attack my patriotism. I was opposed to the war but I love my country." Bush was left flabbergasted as his first attempt to cut down Clinton had completely backfired on him. The first debate concluded with Clinton preserving his lead, Perot establishing his legitimacy and gravitas in going toe to toe over serious issues and Bush failing to do anything that seriously altered the dynamic of the race and giving an overall bland performance.

Two days later in Atlanta, GA the only Vice Presidential debate was held between Vice President Dan Quayle, Senator Al Gore, and Perot's recently named running mate, former Vietnam POW Admiral James Stockdale. Dan Qualye who had been so humiliated in the 1988 Vice Presidential debate with Texas Senator Lloyd Bentsen, "I knew Jack Kennedy" line and been stuck with the lightweight tag ever since gave a surprisingly spirited, coherent and rousing performance attacking Clinton's character and attacking Gore on several policy issues. Gore stuck to refuting Qualye's charges and stayed with the script of espousing positive campaign rhetoric. Gore was well-spoken and well prepared, but this reinforced the image of him as a stiff and wooden policy wonk. Gore and Qualye went back and forth, both landing solid shots but neither got the better of each other. Qualye attempted to use Gore's passion for the environment against him by alleging that Gore planned to use taxpayer dollars to invest in foreign environmental projects, when Gore denied the charge Qualye shot back that Gore's proposal was, "on page 304 of your book" eliciting applause from the audience. Although Qualye's performance saved him from further humiliation and bolstered the spirits of Conservatives, it did little to alter the dynamics of the race.

Two days later, in Richmond, VA, the first-ever town hall-style debate was held where voters could ask direct questions of the candidates. This style had been specifically requested by Governor Clinton, and seeing as how he was leading in all of the polls, the Bush campaign felt it had no choice but to agree to the format. The debate opened on the question of free trade and the impending ratification of the North American Free Trade Agreement (NAFTA). Bush began by stating his support for the treaty by increasing exports while Perot was adamantly against it warning that if it was ratified the United States would hear, "a giant sucking sound of jobs going south". Governor Clinton, as was his forte, gave a more nuanced view by saying that it required more study. The defining moment of the debate came when a young African American woman asked each of the candidates how the national debt had affected them personally. Perot stated that the debt had caused him to drop all of his personal business and get involved in the race. When Bush's turn came, he didn't seem to understand the question that the woman was asking. He went on at length about how he visited an African American Church and how he did not want to have the debt to affect his grandchildren yet failed to give a coherent answer. When his turn finally came, Clinton stood and, giving his most convincing look of empathy, went on to explain at length how, as governor of a small state, he personally knew the people who had lost their jobs when a factory was shipped overseas or when a business went bankrupt. He then pivoted to the reason for the ailing economy was not the debt alone, but the fact that America was invested, "in the grip of a failed economic theory," and rattled off a host of other grim statistics. Afterwards, Clinton campaign strategist James Carville was jubilant, stating that he, "would have paid to have had that question asked." (Hamilton, 2003. p. 678) Bush's cause was not helped by the fact that during the debate, he looked at his watch as if he would rather not be there. With the exception of where he professed amazement at how an electronic scanner worked, this debate, more than anything else, helped to cement the image of Bush as out of touch with ordinary Americans and their concerns.

 A third and final debate was held two days later in East Lansing State, Michigan. At this point President Bush had his back on the wall and had only one last chance to make an impression on a large national audience and change the dynamic of the race. Bush took the attack directly to Clinton, hitting him once again on his character as well as his record as Governor of Arkansas. Bush also kept going after Clinton on his waffling and nuanced statements in regards to just about everything. This was certainly a valid criticism as Clinton had a tendency to try and placate both sides without alienating anyone. Examples of this include his position that NAFTA needed more study and stating that he "didn't inhale" when asked if he had smoked Marijuana as a young man which was convoluted and ambiguous to say the least.

When the topic shifted to foreign policy, Bush's main strength, Perot made the claim that the U.S. had prior knowledge of Saddam Hussein's plans to invade and occupy Kuwait. Bush promptly responded by passionately denying the charge. Bush also got off several good one liners, the first of which was when Clinton attacked Bush for saying that he would put James Baker (his Secretary of State and his current campaign manager) in charge of his economic agenda and then saying that he would put in himself in charge on day one, to which Bush responded to some applause, "That's what worries me." In referring to Perot's leaving the race previously, Bush responded, "If you can't stand the heat, buy an air conditioning company." Bush went on to make the familiar refrain arguing in favor of a line-item veto to cut wasteful spending in bills (pork barrel spending) but again did not offer any specifics on how to revive the economy. Perot took a good bit of flak from Clinton for attacking the condition of Arkansas to which Clinton easily rattled off a list of statistics stating the progress he had made while Governor. Bush closed the debate by once again going back to the character issue. The third debate gave Bush some badly needed momentum as he showed more spunk than he did in the previous two.

Along with the debates, another highlight of October was the advent of Perot's famous infomercials. It goes without saying that Perot had the means to buy up airtime on the major networks in order to promote his philosophy and campaign. Never before had a candidate had the ability (and money) to make his case directly to the American people totally unfiltered. Throughout October millions of viewers were treated to a full hour of nothing but Ross H. Perot talking detailed policy with the aid of dozens of homemade charts containing all kinds of information and statistics. All the while he made these points with a pointer he called his "voodoo stick".

Perot stated plainly what the problems were that the country was facing and how he would deal with them as President. As with his campaign book, United We Stand, he provided lots of detail and specifics backed up by many charts and graphs. To his credit, Perot did not promise not to push for any more tax increases. He stated plainly that he would have to raise taxes and reform entitlements in order to reduce the deficit. Perot proposed a Gasoline tax that would increase 10 cents per year over a five-year period, that he claimed would generate $158 billion in new revenue. (Wilson, 2013) He also promised to crack down on foreign companies and end a whole host of deductions in order to bring in more money. Unlike most politicians, Perot frankly admitted that his proposals would require sacrifice from all Americans, and nobody would be exempt.

On full display were also Perot's witty sayings and homilies. In his last infomercial before the election, Perot attacked Clinton's record as Governor of Arkansas claiming that most of the jobs that had been created in his state were in the poultry industry and if elected, "we would all be plucking chickens for a living". Even more humorously, Perot made the comparison of Arkansas and its budget to the major cities in the U.S. Going even further he brought up a chart that showed where Arkansas would be on the Forbes 500 list if it was a business. According to the chart it would rank 248th (Duncan, 2020) Later on Perot took issue with President Bush's prosecution of the Gulf War stating that most of the objectives listed by the President had not been accomplished. He also attacked the President on the Savings and Loan disaster of the late 1980's, the budget deal with Congress in 1990 and to drive home the perception of Bush being out of touch stated the president "was a man who thought computer chips and potato chips were the same". Perot closed his case by again reiterating that he was in the race because of his love of the country and concern over its course and that unlike the other two candidates he was not owned by lobbyists or corporations. If Americans did not know who would win the election, it could not be said that they did not know Ross H. Perot.

All public figures in the western world are subject to being mocked and ridiculed for their appearance, personality and mannerisms etc. The 1992 campaign was no different, and most memorable are the sketches that were performed on the late-night comedy show Saturday Night Live (SNL) on NBC. As always, they provided a much-needed dose of humor as the campaign wore on. Portraying President Bush and Ross Perot was actor and comedian Dana Carvey. Carvey's sketches of Bush had been on the air for several years throughout his tenures as Vice President and then President. His most well-known impression was of Bush saying, "Not gonna do that. Wouldn't be prudent" in Bush's high pitched nasally voice. Far from being offended by the impersonation of him, President Bush actually was a fan of Carvey's performance and invited him to the White House Christmas Party in December after he had lost the election.

With Perot, Carvey had even more of a field day. In a skit that mocks one his infomercials, Carvey lampoons Perot's supposed hiring of private investigators to spy on his own campaign employees by stating, "I had myself investigated and found out that I have a wife and five children." Another skit mocks a Perot press conference where he claimed that the Republican Party was doctoring photos of his daughter's wedding, playing off Perot's well-known paranoia. In his high pitched, rapid and clipped tone, Carvey shows Perot presenting a doctored picture that supposedly shows his daughter kissing pop singer Madonna. Time and again he is asked by reporters how he knows the photo was altered by "Republican dirty tricks" and each time he obfuscates and accuses the reporters of not listening to him. Exasperated, he finally blurts that the picture is, "as plain as white cotton under panties".

Finally, we see Phil Hartman portraying Bill Clinton at a McDonald's fast-food restaurant being asked questions by voters also ordering food while taking a break from a morning jog. In a nod to Clinton's adultery, when told by the secret service that Mrs. Clinton ordered them not to let him into any more fast-food restaurants, Hartman replies, "There's going to be a whole bunch of things we don't tell Mrs. Clinton, fast food is the least of our worries". Hartman is then asked if he supports the deployment of U.S. troops to famine ridden Somalia. While answering in the affirmative Hartman begins obnoxiously taking food off of customer's trays to illustrate how food being sent to the country is intercepted by Somali warlords and why the deployment is necessary.

Of particular importance in Clinton's victory was the youth vote. Normally the most apathetic voting bloc, the youth vote of 18-24 was unusually engaged throughout the 1992 election cycle. Most of this was due to a record executive who wanted to find a way to get more young people involved in politics. Founded by Jeff Ayeroff in 1990, Rock The Vote was a nonprofit that sought to register young people to help them have a greater voice in the political process. The group gained greater notoriety when it partnered with MTV in order to encourage young people to vote. To spread the message, artists from across the musical spectrum from Sir Mix A lot, Madonna, En Vogue and many others made simple yet heartfelt appeals for young people to use their voice and vote. Before the election there had been a push for legislation termed the

"Motor Voter Law" which would allow anyone getting their license renewed, or getting it for the first time as a sixteen-year-old, to also register to vote. Rock The Vote pushed for the passage of the legislation which had already been vetoed by President Bush. Once he became President, Bill Clinton signed the National Voter Registration Act in May 1993. Rock The Vote was also visible at many music festivals with forms readily available for use by concert goers. Although officially a non-partisan organization, it could not be denied that Rock the Vote and the artists who made their pitch for its cause were happy when Clinton won the election.

As the campaign went down the final stretch, Bush finally appeared to have gained some movement, and his poll numbers rose with a USA Today/Gallup/ CNN poll on October 27, 1992, showing almost a dead heat. (Carville & Matalin, 1994. p. 440) As he made one last sweep across several battleground states, Bush once again hammered on the trust and character issues that had so bedeviled Clinton and seemed to be gaining traction. However all of Bush's late surge momentum immediately evaporated when on October 30, 1992, Independent Counsel Lawrence Walsh issued an indictment against Reagan Defense Secretary Casper Weinberger for false statements relating to his testimony in the Iran Contra scandal of 1986-1987 when officials in the Reagan administration had broken the law by secretly selling weapons to the Iranian regime and then using the proceeds to fund anti-communist Nicaraguan rebels (Contras) in an effort to free American hostages being held in war torn Lebanon. Although a previous indictment had been issued in June and subsequently dismissed from court, Walsh's decision to issue an indictment less than one week away from a national election came under intense scrutiny. The effect on the election was instant, and Bush's poll numbers all but collapsed to the point of erasing any hope of winning.

On Tuesday, November 3, 1992, Americans finally went to the polls to decide who would be the next President. Bush carried 18 states for 168 electoral votes to Clinton's 32 states for 370 electoral votes. Perot received no electoral votes yet pulled in more than 20% of the vote in several states and even came in second place in Maine. Voter turnout had also significantly increased, with 54% of eligible voters equating to roughly 102,060,000 voters out of 189,000,000 people eligible to cast ballots. (Time Editors, 1992, p.49) The results contained several electoral surprises that many would not have thought possible 4 years ago. In the South, where Dukakis, Mondale, and President Carter (save Georgia in 1980) did not even win one state, Clinton managed to win four (Louisiana, Arkansas, Tennessee, and Georgia). Clinton also ended up winning several western states that had not voted Democratic since Lyndon Johnson's landslide victory of 1964, such as Montana, Colorado, and Nevada.

Voting data from different demographics gives great insights into how people voted in the election. According to the Roper Center For Public Opinion Polling, Clinton narrowly carried Men with 41% to Bush's 38% and Perot's 21%. Among Women Clinton's majority was larger with 45% to Bush's 38% to 17% for Perot. In the category of Race Bush won Whites with 41% to Clinton's 39% to Perot's 21%. While among the black population, Clinton won a lopsided victory with 83% to Bush's 10% and Perot's 7%. Clinton dominated among voters between the ages of 18-24 with 46% to Bush's 33% to Perot's 21%. Astonishingly, Clinton swept the age category winning in all recorded age groups although his margin of victory was narrower for some. In a small act of consolation, Bush, despite all his troubles with the right wing of the Republican Party did manage a strong majority among Conservatives with

64% to Clinton's 18% and Perot's 18%. (Ropercenter.cornell.edu/how-groups-voted-1992)

A subject that has long been debated among historians and others, is the question of how many votes Perot took from Clinton and Bush and who his supporters were. It has long been commonplace wisdom and an article of faith among Republicans that many believe Perot cost President Bush re-election. This sentiment has been echoed by the former President himself over the years. In April 2023, a group of polling and political forecasting professionals working for the political analysis organization Split-Ticket.org conducted an interesting study that addressed this very question.

Political analysts Harrison Lavelle and Armin Thomas compiled exit polling data available from 47 states which asked Perot voters who they would have voted for if Perot was not in the race. The data was then compiled excluding Perot voters who would not have voted if he wasn't on the ballot. The results showed that 51% of Perot voters would have voted for Clinton as a second choice and 42% for Bush. The data estimated that Clinton would have won the popular vote 53%-46%, for a comfortable margin of 7%. (Lavell & Thomas, Split-Ticket.org) Although no research and methodology is 100% accurate, this study does give an interesting snap-shot into the minds of Perot voters in the 1992 election. It also makes a convincing argument that Bill Clinton would have won regardless of Perot's presence in the race.

President Bush himself was in shock at the results, having stated and believed that the American people would never elect someone like Bill Clinton. In his hour of defeat, Bush had to have been thinking of the colossal errors he made in breaking his no new taxes pledge from 1988, and his alienation of the Conservatives caused by it. You cannot bite the hand that feeds you and expect to survive, especially in American politics.

It was a lesson that his son and future President George W. Bush was keen to learn from and not repeat.

Clinton's victory was the culmination of the New Democrat philosophy he had pioneered as Chairmen of the Democratic Leadership Council (DLC) of moderating the Democratic Party's liberal rhetoric from 1980's as well as tough hard ball campaigning. Just a mere four years earlier, his election would have been unimaginable for a man with his problems such as the draft issue, philandering and a reputation for being less than honest (hence the Slick Willie moniker). However, like the world events that swept over the globe that made his election possible, the man himself proved to be an insatiable force. Coming back from scandals and political minefields that had destroyed so many other political candidates and still managing to win as the first baby boomer and first President to have not served in World War II in almost 40 years, or the military. A man who simply loved to campaign and talk to as many people as he could, a man who simply enjoyed the endless debate of public policy. The twelve-year reign of Republican Presidents was suddenly gone and a new era in Washington and the country had begun. With the exception of the collapse of the Soviet Union, Clinton's election was the most powerful example of the change that was sweeping the world in the year 1992.

There are so many things that make the 1992 U.S. Presidential Election Campaign stand out in U.S. Presidential history. It was the first presidential election in the modern era where a viable third-party candidate had a chance to win and was allowed to participate in the debates. It was the first election to be held since the end of the Cold War leaving The United States the only remaining superpower on the face of the Earth. Never before had a sitting President who enjoyed the highest approval ratings in the history of polling up until that point suffered a defeat on such a scale. It saw a man whose personal history would have spelled certain defeat four years earlier rise up and overcome tremendous obstacles and crises to become the first Baby Boomer President and the first Democrat to win the White House in sixteen years. As previously stated, never before had a man who had been accused of dodging the draft during the Vietnam War and participating in overseas demonstrations been a viable candidate and winner of the Presidency. It was certainly a first for two political operatives, James Carville and Mary Matalin, from opposing parties to fall in love and later marry. Also, in a lot of ways it was the most humorous election from the personalities of Perot, Clinton, Bush, the infomercials, the one-liners, parody skits and zingers in the debates etc. The election was not just about politics, policy and personality, it was also entertainment. The 1992 U.S. Presidential election will be remembered as many things, but forgettable will never be one of them.

1992

After a shocking fall from an approval rating of 91% following the end of the Gulf War, President Bush had to campaign against a recession, a primary challenge from Patrick Buchannan and the man from Hope. It simply proved to be too much.

The inclusion of Third-Party candidate Ross Perot provided an unprecedented aspect to the Presidential debates held in October 1992.

Billionaire Ross Perot tapped into the electorate's discontent with the two-party system and business as usual. His vast wealth enabled him to run his campaign as he saw fit. His free-wheeling personality garnered him plenty of attention and publicity.

Arkansas Gov. Bill Clinton ran a dynamic, energetic, and sometimes problematic race for the democratic nomination in 1992. He surprised pundits by selecting another southerner, Tennessee Senator AL Gore Jr., as his running mate.

CHAPTER 3

The Seattle Sonic Boom and the Riff Heard Round the World

In early 1988, an obscure band played their first show in the capital of Washington State, Olympia. Their first show had been over a year ago in Raymond, W.A., at a house party. Olympia was also a college town, home to Evergreen State University and despite its reputation for hippie liberalism there was also an element of cliquish snobbery that is present in most University settings. The band was called Nirvana, and the leader Kurt Donald Cobain was following his dream of playing music and being a rock and roll star. Formed just over a year ago in early 1987, they had played mainly house parties, radio shows and a few concerts. Despite being a new band, it was evident that there was something special about the group. Cobain's girlfriend at the time, Tracy Marander, had stated when she heard them play, "My mouth dropped open, these guys were good." (Cross, 2019, p.95) There was an unusual intensity and ferocity about the band's performances and Cobain's voice in particular. However, this evening they were to find out how the very same people who professed tolerance and acceptance could be just as dismissive and condescending as any group who didn't fully accept those as not of their own. As the band was setting up, one attendee grabbed the microphone and blurted out, "Drummers from Aberdeen (W.A.) sure look weird." (Cross, 2019, p.101) Although the remark was made in reference to current drummer Dave Foster, it could have just easily applied to the whole band. And it cut deeply. Even as outsiders in the so called "grunge" scene the band and Cobain in particular learned they still had to act and dress a certain part.

Perhaps the most profound and far-reaching change in the music world ever (with the possible exception of the British invasion of 1964) occurred in the early 1990s. It was when the 1991-1992 grunge rock movement gathered momentum and burst into the mainstream of popular culture. The man who was most responsible for bringing about that change was the last person who wanted large-scale fame and notoriety. That, of course, being one Kurt Donald Cobain. Nevertheless, Nirvana, Pearl Jam, Dinosaur Jr., Mudhoney, Sonic Youth, Sound Garden, Smashing Pumpkins, and many more led the charge out of the 1980s hair/glam rock and into the angst-filled 1990s. Along with these artists came a series of albums that shook up the music industry to its bones in substance and quality that the industry has not seen since. Pearl Jam's Ten, Alice in Chains' *Facelift*, and, of course, Nirvana's *Nevermind*, which started the whole bonfire. Like most other musical eras, the movement had its own fashions, the ever-present long hair and flannel shirts being the most memorable, but unlike bands of the past decade, these bands actually spoke and stood for something. A generation that had no Vietnams, no Civil Rights struggle, seemed to yell out in frustration as opposed to outrage, "What are we here for and what is our purpose!!??

The voice of the generation had been brewing for a long time throughout the 1980s in underground club scenes throughout the Pacific Northwest, but mainly in Seattle, Washington. Mudhoney, Soundgarden, The Melvins, Screaming Trees, or Nirvana, all those names would not have registered with hardly anyone outside the aforementioned Seattle club scene in 1989. However, within the next two years, almost anyone who watched MTV or listened to rock music would not be able to escape their existence. To attribute the entire grunge movement to Kurt Cobain is an honor the man would have vehemently rejected. Cobain himself often pointed out that there were better bands out there than his and deserved more recognition, and yet the movement would never have happened without him. One has only to look at man's upbringing, surroundings, and his past to discover the resonance his music touched off in his generation.

It goes without saying that social and societal forces played a very significant role in the rise of the grunge movement as much as the musical landscape of the 1980's did. Throughout the 1970's the divorce rate had risen sharply throughout the nation and the story of Cobain's family is one that played out in countless homes across the U.S. It is indeed striking to note that out of the 5 lead singers of the major bands associated with grunge (Kurt Cobain, Eddie Vedder, Layne Staley, Chris Cornell and Billy Corgan), all their parents divorced when they were at a young age. All of them would also struggle with some form of domestic or substance abuse and all save Billy Corgan would drop out of High School. Sadly, as of this writing, only two of these singers, Vedder and Corgan, are still alive. Staley died from a drug overdose in April 2002. Cobain and Cornell having both committed suicide in 1994 and 2017 respectively. His death was a mortal wound to the movement that divides the before and after.

Kurt Donald Cobain was born on February 20, 1967, to Wendy and Donald Cobain. When Cobain was just 8 years old, his parents divorced, and young Kurt's world was thrown into upheaval. Cobain's parents both remarried and he found it increasingly difficult to adapt to having other children in his family to compete with for parental attention and affection.

Over the years, Cobain bounced around from mother, father, other family, and friends, etc. Cobain's anger towards his parents would manifest itself in his refusal to get along with other students and intentionally failing at sports in order to spite his father. One example of this would be Cobain allegedly allowing himself to be pinned in wrestling matches in junior high. (Cross, 2019, p.37-38) Cobain would cite his parent's divorce as having a profound impact on his life saying that he felt ashamed that he did not have the typical American family household to come home to.

After dropping out of high school in 1985 and several periods of being homeless, Cobain honed his passion for music and art. Cobain would delve into the punk rock scene of the Seattle area and form his first band, Fecal Matter. After only one-year, Fecal Matter was disbanded, and Cobain began hanging out in the practice area of another punk band named the Melvins. The Melvins had a tremendous influence on Cobain's musical development and taste. Lead singer and guitarist Buzz Osborne (aka King Buzzo) exposed Cobain to many bands and musical styles. Hardcore punk band Black Flag being a major source of inspiration. The band experimented with a variety of styles such as Sludge Rock, Hardcore punk etc. and was truly on the fringe musically and culturally. For a time, Cobain would even drive the Melvins tour van when they went on tour. While doing so, Cobain would meet Krist Novoselic and the two formed Nirvana in early 1987. The band went through several drummers, none of which lasted too long before settling on Chad Channing with whom they would record their first album, *Bleach*, in 1989.

If ever there was an instance where a band was "underground," Nirvana and many other bands in the late 1980s and early 1990s fit that description. The very term grunge brings to mind something slow-moving and sludgy, which is exactly how Nirvana's first album could be described.

The grunge movement was confined to the northwest of Washington State in bars, garages, and other places that would let them play for little or no money. The grunge sound began to gather steam due to the independent record label Sub Pop. That sound could be described simply as a shotgun marriage of punk rock from the late 70's and metal from the 80's, with a stronger emphasis on lyrics and songwriting than the former and latter. Without the Sub Pop record label, it is unlikely that grunge would have been able to break into the mainstream and achieve success. Sub Pop was founded in 1986 by Bruce Pavit and Jonathan Poneman and was responsible for signing many groups, such as Soundgarden, Sonic Youth, and Mudhoney, to name a few, that later became famous in the grunge era. Sub Pop would also start a subscription service that would allow subscribers to purchase artist singles via mail and help give exposure to countless folks in the Indie (Independent Record Label) realm. The genius of Poneman and Pavit was in their foresight to fashion what became known as the "Seattle Sound," which gave the music a regional flavor in the same vein as Motown did for R&B in the early to mid-1960s.

In 1988, the label released Sub Pop 200, which was a compilation of its current artists. Nirvana appears on the album with a song called "Spank-Thru" that features many classic Nirvana characteristics. Along with Kurt's howling vocals, there is also the hard charging guitar solo and the typical band sound of high intensity. More obscure artists such as Beat Happening, Blood Circus, Tad, and even shock poet Jesse Bernstein make appearances along with better-known ones such as Soundgarden and Green River. Although *Sub Pop 200* was not widely available at the time of its release, it does provide a rich insight into the "Seattle sounds" beginnings and development.

Sonic Youth, in particular, had a profound impact on the development and breakout of grunge both artistically and commercially.

Formed in 1981 in New York City and a whole continent away from Seattle, the group was the brainchild of Thurston Moore and Kim Gordon, who played guitar and bass, respectively. Throughout the 1980 s, the group became very influential in the indie scene in NYC and pioneered what became known as the noise rock/no-wave musical genre. With heavily distorted guitar arrangements and a highly unconventional sound, the band built a cult following and released five albums throughout the 1980s on SST and other indie labels. The band's decision to sign with major record label DGC in 1989 demonstrated to many, Cobain in particular, that an underground band could go mainstream without compromising their music and ideals.

In 1989, Nirvana's first album, *Bleach,* was released on Sub Pop and was well received, but did not sell in great numbers due to the independent underground nature of Sub Pop. This is mainly distribution capability and promotion. Poneman and Pavit would adopt a marketing strategy of pressing only a limited number of records for an artist to help fuel demand. A strategy adopted by many other indie music labels. When *Bleach* was re-released in 1992, after the success of *Nevermind*, its sales began to pick up a great deal. *Bleach* was much as its title suggested, very bleak, slow, and gave one a feeling of being in sludge, the exception being the Beatlesque "About A Girl". Over the next two years, Nirvana would continue touring as well as writing new material for their next album, which would catapult them into mainstream success and radically alter the state of music.

Although the explosion of *Nevermind* has been cited as when grunge became fully mainstream, it is important to remember that other artists from the Seattle area had started to achieve some commercial success. Soundgarden, formed in 1984, had already released two full-length LPs, *Ultramega OK* (1988) and *Louder Than Love* (1989), as well as two EPs.

They had even signed to a major label (A&M Records) by the time of their second LP. Across the country in Chicago, IL, The Smashing Pumpkins had released their debut album *Gish* in May 1991 on Caroline Records. Although *Gish* would only go platinum after the release of 1993's Siamese Dream, it would still become one of the best-selling independent records at the time. *Gish* was also notable because it was produced by Butch Vig who would then go on to produce *Nevermind*. It is also worth noting that R.E.M., although not considered grunge per se, whose album *Out of Time* had hit number 1 on Billboard charts in May 1991, proved that there was a growing market for alternative bands on the horizon. Alice In Chains became the first group of the emerging genre to have a gold record when the group's debut album *Facelift*, released in August of 1990, was certified as such on September 11, 1991. Although it took *Facelift* just over a year to go Gold, *Nevermind* would reach not only this benchmark in just over two months after its release but also go platinum as well on November 27, 1991. (riaa.com/gold and platinum)

The breakthrough for Nirvana came at the end of 1990 when Cobain, who was unsatisfied with the lack of promotion on behalf of *Bleach*, began to look for a major record label to sign with as well as find a new drummer to replace Chad Channing with whose drumming Cobain had become disenchanted with. Throughout 1990, Nirvana had begun to attract attention from major record labels and, heeding the advice of friends from the band Sonic Youth, had decided to sign with DGC (David Geffen Company) records in April 1991 and begin work on their follow-up album, *Nevermind*. Sonic Youth's first major label record, Goo, released in June 1990, had sold over 200,000 copies. This would play a major role in Cobain's decision to sign with DGC. As the band's sound began to evolve, Cobain and Novoselic felt that Channing's drumming was inadequate to match this change, and he was forced out of the band

and replaced by Dave Grohl, whose drumming was more intense and punk driven. Recording for *Nevermind* began in May and lasted until June 1991. The record was produced by Butch Vig who worked well with the band.

On September 24, 1991, the second studio album of Nirvana, *Nevermind,* was released and shipped to stores around the country, and it immediately began to sell at a very rapid rate. The marketing strategy of DCG Records had been that if the band and management all worked diligently and hard that the record could be certified gold within one year. However, due to such strong sales, the record reached gold status within less than two months of release. *Nevermind* first charted on the Billboard 200 on October 12, 1991, at #144 and went Gold (certified 500,000 copies sold) on October 29. (riaa.com/gold-platinum and gold) In a month, the band went from national obscurity to global super-stardom, almost unprecedented in music history. Even Michael Jackson started in the Jackson Five. *Nevermind's* climb up the charts was also accompanied by a change in the band's fan base at concerts. As an Indie (Independent) band, Nirvana had played to crowds mostly attuned specifically to the punk rock scene. As their success and recognition skyrocketed, more and more members of the audience were made up of the very people that Nirvana professed to hate such as Jocks, Rednecks and the Bullies. As their popularity grew, so did the accusations of "selling out" from indie scene purists. This dichotomy would define Nirvana's success and other grunge artists as well.

To fully grasp the success of *Nevermind,* it helps to have at least a cursory understanding of the landscape of the music industry at the time of its release. For the last week of September 1990, exactly one year before *Nevermind's* release, the top 3 albums on the Billboard 200 were #1. M.C. Hammer's *Please Don't Hurt' Em,* followed by Wilson Phillips self-titled album at #2, and Mariah Carey also self-titled album at #3. The closest album that could be considered alternative was Jane's Addiction's *Ritual De Lo Habitual* at #24. (www. Billboard.com/charts/billboard-200) The Billboard Hot 100 (which tracks singles) was dominated by Pop, Rhythm and Blues, and Dance-oriented groups with a smattering of Glam Rock bands such as Poison and solo artists such as Jon Bon Jovi. The #1 spot was held by a dance trio called Sweet Sensation with their single "If Wishes Come True". (www. Billboard.com/charts/hot-100/) In short, the airwaves were dominated by musicians who had either been around for a long time, such as Phil Collins, or were simple pop acts unlikely to have any longevity, such as Color Me Badd. The atmosphere was ripe for anyone, anything, or any band, for that matter, to connect with young people with a message that resonated and exploded.

The rapid success of *Nevermind* was due in large part to the airing on MTV of the first single from the album, "Smells Like Teen Spirit." The constant airing and newfound success were beyond overwhelming for the group. The band, which was used to playing indoor concerts for maybe 1,000-2,000 people, found out that all of a sudden their concerts were sold out with people desperate to see them, as well as a larger than usual contingent of TV cameras on stage with them and also during performances. As the band toured across Europe in the fall of 1991, they found that every country they went to wanted a TV interview as well as concert footage of them performing, and due to the close proximity of countries in Europe the band denying one interview to one station could leave that country without a Nirvana interview. (Azerrad, 1993, p.204) On top of their new superstar status, touring and press coverage, the band and Cobain were becoming exhausted. It was during this time that Cobain's use of Heroin began to become an issue of speculation in the press.

The powerful primal force of *Nevermind* was hitting the public consciousness (and record stores) with the force of a thousand Atomic Bombs. To appreciate the album's impact, one must understand the powerful, primal force that drives the album itself. To quote what Rolling Stone writer Ira Robbins wrote of *Nevermind's* sound, it was, "a dynamic mix of sizzling power chords, manic energy and sonic restraint, Nirvana erects sturdy melodic structures but then attacks them with frenzied screaming and guitar havoc." (Robbins/Editors, 1994, p.20) The album starts with the universally known guitar chords of "Smells Like Teen Spirit" crashing onto one's ears, continues with the slower but just as powerful "In Bloom", descends into the watery and melodramatic "Come As You Are", picks back up the pace with "Breed" followed by the painful "Lithium" and concludes on side one with the slow and tortuous "Polly". Side two starts out roaring with the explosive "Territorial Pissings", then the Zeppelin Esque "Drain You", followed by the odd "Lounge Act", then the angry "Stay Away", the profound " On a Plain" and finally finishes off with the slow moving and sad "Something In The Way" which Cobain claimed was about when he was homeless living under a bridge in Aberdeen. After ten minutes or so of silence, the listener is treated to the feedback-driven harsh instrumental of "Endless Nameless". And after the piercing feedback finally fades (for real this time), the listener is finally left to sit in silence, processing the 43-minute wall of sound produced by the trio, or flip back to Side 1 and listen again. *Nevermind* is loud and quiet and fast and slow. It is dynamic, exuberant, awkward, and angsty, just like youth.

The entrance of grunge into the mainstream became undeniable when, in January of 1992, *Nevermind* knocked off Michael Jackson's *Dangerous* from the number one spot on the Billboard Top 200 album charts. This feat was followed by two high-profile performances. This would be America's first exposure to Nirvana as a live act, as most people at this point knew of them mainly through *Nevermind* and the Teen Spirit video. The first was a taped recording for MTV's 120 Minutes on January 10, where the band performed seven tracks in front of a studio audience. The second was an appearance on Saturday Night Live (SNL) the next evening. The band played two tracks, "Smells Like Teen Spirit" and, unexpectedly, "Territorial Pissings". Both performances showed the band in top form, with the SNL appearance ending with the usual instrument smashing and set demolition. Despite Cobain's almost overdosing on heroin before the SNL performance, it was a raw display of their ferocity and power.

No more was grunge merely a flash in the pan with a bunch of guys wearing ratty clothing; now it was a national movement and a major commercial force. Seattle area bands were now signing to major record labels in droves and raking in big bucks. Major fashion companies were now producing grunge-like clothing and marketing it to the public. "Nirvana-mania" was everywhere as critics and fans debated the meaning of Cobain's lyrics. A February 1992 cover of Rolling Stone magazine even featured the cast of the Teen Drama Beverly Hills 90210 show with the title cover "Smells Like Teen Spirit," much to the displeasure of the band. The major record labels were all now convinced that the next biggest cash cow lay within the grunge movement. The movement even spread to film and fashion when on September 18, 1992, filmmaker and writer Cameron Crowe released a film called Singles that depicts the romantic life of several young members of Generation X (those born from 1965-1980), in and around Seattle at the height of the grunge movement. The plot itself did not contain anything novel, but it did signal the cultural phenomenon of grunge transcending simply the music industry. It also didn't hurt that several high-profile grunge musicians made appearances on the soundtrack, ranging from Pearl Jam, Soundgarden, and the Smashing Pumpkins, to name a few. The stereotypical flannel sweaters, long hair, and carefree attitude of youth are all portrayed with light-hearted humor and charm. Even a fictitious band called Citizen Dick, with guest appearances by Eddie Vedder, Jeff Ament and Stone Gossard of the real-life band Pearl Jam as band members, take one into the supposed workings of a grunge band on the make.

Being suddenly thrust into the mainstream and the scrutiny of the limelight was hard for grunge's central figures. The high regard for authenticity and the cardinal sins of being a poseur or sell-out made stardom a bitter pill to swallow for most. For Cobain, the change in concert attendance, from punk outsiders to mainstream America, was met with a discomfort that often leaned towards contempt. He would always struggle with the fact that people who would have never shown up for a Nirvana concert prior to *Nevermind* were suddenly attending shows. It was felt by Kurt and the band that these people were not true fans and just merely jumping on the bandwagon for as long as it was deemed cool by the media and MTV. (Azerrad, 1993, p. 199-200) Success and fan resentment were the least of Cobain's worries as he and his wife, Courtney Love's daughter (Francis Bean Cobain, who was born in August of 1992) were stripped of their custody after it was alleged in a Vanity Fair article that Love used drugs while pregnant with Francis. Although full custody was eventually restored to the couple, the episode took its toll on Cobain and Love.

Yet with success came some degree of influence and power. At least as far as music festivals go. On August 30, 1992, Nirvana played what was perhaps their greatest performance at the Reading Festival in the U.K. Amid the swirling rumors of drug addiction, custody battles, and the band breaking up, Nirvana delivered an exhilarating concert. The roster of artists had more or less been selected by Cobain who had stated that Nirvana would not play if the organizers refused to schedule the bands he wanted such as the Melvins and L7 etc. (Cross, 2019, p.251) Playing off the press speculation of heroin abuse, Cobain was rolled out onto the stage in a wheelchair by bassist Kris Novoselic and dressed in a hospital gown and a ratty blonde wig. Krist Novoselic spoke into the mic, "It's too painful… you're gonna make it, man…with the support of his friends and family, he's gonna make it." Unsteady and frail, Kurt pulled himself up to the microphone. He sang a few lines from Bette Midler's "The Rose" and collapsed, flat on his back. After a brief moment, Cobain got up nonchalantly, took a guitar from a tech, and the band launched into a full-fledged sonic assault to silence their critics. Playing a total of twenty-five songs, complete with the usual instrument smashing and set demolition, the band showed they were alive and kicking. There was even on-stage banter between the band about making a new album and how it was not their last show. Towards the end of the show, Cobain playfully made a heartfelt plea for the audience to shout, "Courtney, we love you!!" in response to all the negative press she and Cobain had been subjected to. The show ended with Cobain doing a distorted and tortured version of the National Anthem before handing his guitar off to the crowd as a coveted souvenir.

The rise of grunge also sparked some clashes with musicians outside of the grunge orbit. The 1992 MTV Video Music Awards, held on September 9, 1992, was where things came to a head between the band and Axl Rose of Guns N' Roses. The ascent of grunge was called "the nail in the coffin of the hair metal era" and could be said in large part to have affected the career of bands such as Guns N' Roses. Artistic differences aside, Rose made plain that he did not like Nirvana and Cobain personally after failing to get Nirvana to tour with them. While backstage at the music awards Love jokingly asked Rose whether or not he would be her child's godfather to which Rose, who happened to be surrounded by a security entourage, pointed his finger at Cobain and allegedly said, "You shut your bitch up or I'm taking you down to the pavement." This ugly incident was retold by Cobain humorously in later interviews. There was tension not just from other music genres but also from other grunge bands. Pearl Jam's Eddie Vedder and Cobain had also feuded over the past year. Cobain believed that Pearl Jam was not an authentic product of the grunge revolution and that they were, "pioneering a corporate, alternative cock rock fusion." (Azerrad/ Editors, 1994, p. 35) This rivalry might sound a bit surprising, considering that both bands faced intense media scrutiny and felt the pressure of the generational spokesman label. Both men were also outspoken pro-choice and progressive politics advocates. Both also gave unusually intense live performances with Vedder's cathartic gyrations and Cobain's howling and instrument smashing . Being a small and insular scene, Seattle bands regularly worked together. The tight knit community of musicians formed various short-lived groups and one-off projects together. As majorly successful bands, they continued to feature each other as guests on recordings and onstage. There may have been a sense of competition between bands, but grunge was fundamentally grounded in mutual support. The success of the Seattle scene was a collective endeavor. And despite their rivalry, Cobain would often admit to liking Vedder personally.

Nirvana's breakthrough onto the music scene in late 1991, early 1992 helped to galvanize a generation but also fundamentally remade not only rock music, but the music industry as well. Grunge established the commercial viability of alternative rock music, which, after a decade of 1980s metal/ hair bands, had substance and resonated with people. Perhaps the greatest irony of all is that, in contrast to many bands that came before them, becoming super famous and rich was the last thing on Cobain's agenda. As with any underground concept that becomes famous, there follow the inevitable accusations of selling out in order to make a buck. It was no surprise that Nirvana's follow-up album to *Nevermind* was the complete opposite of what most critics and fans were expecting. The harsh distortion of *In Utero*, released in the fall of 1993, took many by surprise. The album was so raw and unrefined that at first, DGC didn't think the album would be commercially viable. (Goldberg, 2019, p. 220) The songs on the album convey a distinct feeling of fatigue and disgust with fame and the limelight. *Utero's* producer Steve Albini sought to produce a record that sounded the exact opposite of *Nevermind* and wildly succeeded, although the band would bring in Scott Litt of R.E.M. to do some touch-up work on the record's sound. Upon its release, In Utero would go on to critical and commercial acclaim.

After the release of *In Utero*, Nirvana would embark on a U.S. and European tour. Cobain's heroin problem would come to a head in March of 1994, when, while on tour initially, he overdosed and briefly fell into a coma from which he recovered. Upon returning to the United States, Love and several other friends convinced Cobain to seek treatment for his out-of-control Heroin Addiction. Cobain flew down to Los Angeles to check himself into a drug rehabilitation program, only to escape after two days and fly back to Seattle on March 30, 1994. After several days of being spotted around town at various locations, Cobain was found dead in an upstairs room over his garage on April 8, 1994, from a self-inflicted gunshot wound to the head. Cobain's death signaled the end of the main phase of the grunge revolution. What followed was "radio-friendly" alternative music that, while still possessing some level of resonance and introspection, did not possess any underground roots. Bands like Bush and Silverchair were synthetic approximations of the genuine article. Still,

Cobain made a significant contribution to making alternative music mainstream and viable commercially. It is perhaps a most extreme irony that in giving a voice to a generation and forever altering the musical landscape, the very thing Cobain sought to avoid became an inescapable reality. He became famous and, in doing so, proved that one voice, however tortured and angry, can bring change and make a difference. By going against the grain, you can become the grain and effect change, even if that was not Cobain's intention.

As significant as Nirvana's *Nevermind* was to the grunge explosion, another group also broke into the mainstream in 1992 and had just as big an impact. Bass player Jeff Amet and guitarist Stone Gossard had already been involved with two groups of major significance to the Seattle scene. Those groups are Green River and Mother Love Bone. The first group had moderate success with two EPs and one LP while they were active as a band from 1984 to 1988. Their first EP, *Come on Down*, was released in 1985 and is widely considered to be the first grunge album ever. The group would experience tensions within the band over what direction they should take going forward. Both Amet and Gossard wanted to sign with a major label in order to increase their visibility. While the group's lead singer, Mark Arm, wanted them to remain strictly an indie underground band. The group would break up in 1988 with Arm going on to found Mudhoney. Amet and Gossard's next group would be on the verge of a commercial and critical breakthrough when, as so often in the music world, tragedy would strike in the form of a drug overdose. Mother Love Bone is significant in several ways, in the sense that it was arguably the first grunge group with a charismatic and visible frontman. For a while, it seemed that one Andrew Patrick Wood was destined to break out and achieve fame and recognition.

Born January 8, 1966, from a young age, Wood was musically inclined and learned to play the piano, keyboard, and guitar as well. In 1980, at only just 14 years old, he formed his first band, the cleverly named Malfunkshun. Although they never released a full-length album until their breakup, Malfunkshun appeared on the first grunge compilation album called *Deep 6,* released in April 1986 on C/Z Records. Like *Sub Pop 200, Deep 6* had a variety of songs from the burgeoning Seattle scene, such as Soundgarden, Skin Yard, The Melvins, and Green River, in addition to Malfunkun. The band broke up in 1988, and Wood would go on to form Mother Love Bone with Amet and Gossard. During their two years as a band (1988-1990), the group would release one EP, *Shine,* in 1989, and complete their only full-length album, *Apple,* before Wood's death on March 19, 1990.

Apple would not be released until July 19, 1990, four months after Wood's death from a heroin overdose. Wood's charisma on and off the stage had led many to speculate that Mother Love Bone would be the first grunge band to have major commercial success and reach a large audience outside the Pacific N.W. Wood had a persona that was similar in some ways to Guns N' Roses frontman Axl Rose, as he also played the piano/keyboard. Wood's death devastated the surviving members of the band and the Seattle music community. Amet and Gossard, along with their friend guitarist Mike McCreedy, would team up with Soundgarden frontman Chris Cornell and drummer Matt Cameron to form a one-time group, Temple of the Dog, to honor Wood. The group released a self-titled album on April 16, 1991, on A&M Records. *Temple of the Dog* was significant in several ways. It is at once melodic and yet powerful. The title of the group had been taken from the lyrics of one of Mother Love Bone's songs, "Man of Golden Words's." Songs such as "Say Hello 2 Heaven", "Reach Down", and "Hunger Strike" were especially moving and evocative of Wood's memory. The latter song was of particular significance because it featured the first major appearance of one Eddie Jerome Vedder on co-lead vocals with Cornell. At the same time Temple of the Dog was released, Amet Gossard had already formed another band and recruited Vedder as the lead singer. The name of the new group formed in the fall of 1990 was initially named after Mookie Blaylock, who at the time was a famous Basketball player in the NBA. Due to potential legal issues, they soon changed their name to the now world-famous Pearl Jam.

Born on December 23, 1964, to Karen Lee Vedder and Edward Louis Severson Jr., Edward Louis Severson III's early life and childhood were in many ways typical of those belonging to Generation X. The family hailed from Evanston,Ill. When Severson was less than a year old, his parents divorced, and his mother remarried shortly after to a man by the name of Peter Mueller. For many years, Edward believed that his stepfather was his biological father until he learned who his real father was. It was only then that he decided to change his last name to his mother's maiden name. Like almost all his contemporaries, Vedder was drawn to and took solace in music at an early age. When Vedder was around ten, his family moved to San Diego, and for his 12th birthday, he received a guitar. Vedder has stated on many occasions that the Who's double album *Quadrophenia* was a source of great inspiration and comfort to him throughout these years. Unlike Cobain, however, Vedder did not appear to be bullied or get seriously involved with drugs. While Vedder was in High School, his mother divorced Mueller and moved back to Illinois with his younger siblings while Vedder stayed behind in San Diego with his stepfather. Shortly thereafter, Vedder moved out on his own and began working during his senior year of High School. Soon, he would drop out and move back to Illinois and earn his G.E.D. from a community college while working a series of odd jobs to support himself.

In 1984, Vedder decided to move back out to the San Diego area, and it was during this time that he began to record demos and play in various local bands. In 1988, he would become the lead singer for a band called Bad Radio, and although they would never release or record music, they would become well-known throughout Southern California. Vedder eventually befriended former Red Hot Chili Peppers drummer Jack Irons and, through him, would receive a demo tape in mid-1990 from Amet and Gossard in Seattle, who were seeking a new singer for a band they had yet to form. While Vedder was surfing one day (his other main hobby), he wrote lyrics for the three demo songs. Upon recording them, he mailed the demo tape with completed lyrics back to Amet in Seattle. Amet and Gossard were so blown away by Vedder's voice that they invited him to come to Seattle and audition in person. Upon arriving at the airport, Vedder requested to immediately get to work recording, to which Amet and Gossard agreed. Upon seeing Vedder perform in person, they were even more impressed with his stage presence. Like Cobain, Vedder's performances were energetic, emotional, and at times manic, but always captivating. Although he was capable of playing guitar, Vedder was mainly a vocalist in the early years of the group. Immediately, Amet and Gossard knew that their search was over and that they had found their man.

By September 1990, the band initially known as Mookie Blaylock was now fully formed. In addition to Eddie Vedder as their lead vocalist, they added Gossard's friend and fellow guitarist Mike McCready and Dave Krusen on drums. Just after the band's formation, they were also working with Chris Cornell on the side project Temple of the Dog while also getting their bearings as a new band, writing and recording new material. As stated previously, Vedder's co-lead vocals with Cornell were his first recorded appearances. Mookie Blaylock's first show with Vedder occurred on October 22, 1990, at the Off Ramp in Seattle. Almost as soon as they formed, the group began working on their debut album, which would be called *Ten* and happened to be Blaylock's jersey number. In contrast with Nirvana, the members of Pearl Jam were avid basketball and sports fans. Amet himself had been a star athlete in High School, and Vedder would shoot hoops occasionally also.

Ten was recorded in just over a month from March through April in 1991. Around the same time, the group signed a major label deal with Epic Records. Just before the recording of *Ten* began, the band announced that they were changing their name officially to Pearl Jam, as being named after a living person, let alone a famous basketball player, carried potential legal issues. The songs on the album reflected many themes that were common among Generation X, such as abuse, loneliness, bullying, and love gone sour. It was on these tracks that the chemistry of the group really came together.

The opening track, "Once," starts with a mellow intro followed by a guitar blast and does not let up for the rest of the song. It tells the story of a man driven by madness into becoming a serial killer. The pace keeps up on "Even Flow," which shows the world from the perspective of a homeless man shunned by society and suffering from mental illness. Quotes such as "Rests his head on a pillow made of concrete" drive home the reality of the man's plight. "Alive," which oddly enough has tons of Oedipus Rex, is about a young boy who bears an uncanny resemblance to his deceased father. His mother then falls in love with him due to the resemblance and has an inappropriate relationship with him. "She walks slowly across a young man's room. She says I'm ready. For you". A fact that no doubt was missed by many fans at the time of the song's release.

"Why Go" delves into the dark world of a young woman institutionalized for no reason and destroyed mentally as a result. It is a sad testimonial to parents who think their child has a problem when they, in fact, are the problem. It is a hard rocker that keeps a fast tempo throughout. The pace drops briefly at the beginning of the iconic "Black" as Vedder painfully describes the emotions swirling around a lost love. The song builds in intensity and crescendos with the searing line, "I know someday you'll have a beautiful life. I know you'll be a sun in somebody else's sky. But why why why couldn't it be mine?"

Next up is the pen-ultimate "Jeremy," which tells the painstaking story of a young boy who is bullied and neglected to the point where he commits suicide in his classroom at school, and as will be discussed shortly, was probably their most powerful music video. Then comes the contemplative and expansive "Oceans," which would be made into one of their few music videos, also notable for the rare use of Timpani drums. The explosive fan favorite "Porch" comes next, which includes a solo interlude that Vedder would use to engage in his stage/rigging climbing antics. The exact meaning of the song is ambiguous, and Vedder has never given a direct answer as to what it's about. Some have speculated that it is about abortion as Vedder handwritten "pro-choice" on his arm during the MTV Unplugged taping. "Garden," which rounds out track nine, is a slow, brooding number followed by the last rocker of the album, "Deep". The album ends with the meandering and slow "Release" and fades out with the same music heard during the intro on the first track. Vedder's soaring voice and lyrics, combined with Ament's bass playing and McCreddy and Gossard's guitar combo, all made for a powerful and compelling tandem throughout the album.

Ten was released on August 27, 1991, almost a full month before Nirvana's *Nevermind*. Four days prior, on August 23, the band played a free concert at Seattle's Mural Amphitheatre right behind the world-famous Space Needle. Ironically, it was also the same date that Nirvana was playing the Reading festival in the U.K., half a world away. The concert showcases the live chemistry between the band members and, most importantly, Vedder's powerful stage presence from the body gyrations, hand gestures, and microphone swinging (skillfully done so as not to hit anyone). And like his hero, The Who frontman Roger Daltrey, Vedder swung the mic around with seemingly reckless abandon. One other stage antic that would come along shortly and demonstrate the passion, and some would say reckless disregard, of Vedder would be his stage climbing during the song "Porch". During the guitar solo of the song, which often turns into an extended guitar jam/ medley, Vedder, in a trance-like state, would climb up the rigging of the stages Pearl Jam would be playing on. At times, this would cause great alarm among the fans and his bandmates. As a live band, Pearl Jam is precise and in tune with each other. Their improvisation shows a collection of musicians who are masters of their instruments. Their performances include audience sing-alongs and banter between the band and the crowd. No one can doubt the sincerity and authenticity of Vedder and the band's passion and the feelings behind their songs, and the emotions they stir.

If Nirvana's *Nevermind* was equivalent to a nuclear explosion in the music industry, Pearl Jam's *Ten* was like a slow-burning fuse on a massive powder keg. The record did not immediately chart or sell in great numbers. Yet in late 1991 and throughout all of 1992, the album would begin to pick up steam with the singles "Alive", "Even Flow", and "Jeremy". As will be discussed shortly, the latter song and the music video greatly increased the band's visibility and popularity, as well as their intense live performances. Vedder may have been known as shy and somewhat avoidant, but he was also charismatic and very likable, which didn't hurt.

On March 16, 1992, Pearl Jam performed on M.T. V's *Unplugged* show, which per the show's intention, showed the band's softer side. One month later, on April 11, they were on Saturday Night Live giving another blistering performance with "Alive" and "Porch". On June 8, another high-profile performance followed at the Pinkpop Festival in the Netherlands that saw the band playing for an audience of over 60,000 and saw Vedder stage dive during the usual extended version of Porch. Finally, there was the 1992 MTV Video Music Awards on September 9 in Los Angeles, where the band played "Jeremy". It was also at the MTV awards show where Kurt Cobain and Eddie Vedder reconciled by slow dancing during Eric Clapton's "Tears in Heaven". Cobain allegedly told Vedder that he respected him as a person, even if he did not like his music. (Azerrad, 1993, p. 279) It could be said that this small encounter, however brief, finally put to rest the feud between two of the biggest bands in the grunge scene that, in retrospect, seemed pointless given how alike the two men were. Throughout the rest of the year, *Ten* would continue to sell millions of copies, and Pearl Jam, along with Nirvana, would continue to dominate the airwaves. However, it was in the video medium that both bands truly reached stratospheric levels in terms of cultural significance, as well as further drive the record sales of their music.

As the grunge wave continued to roll through 1992, other grunge and alternative bands also began to have major commercial success. Many of them had also been prominent fixtures in the Seattle scene for just as long, if not longer than Nirvana. Alice In Chains, whose album *Facelift* had been the first alternative record to achieve gold status, had a very productive and successful 1992. Formed in 1987 by guitarist and songwriter Jerry Cantrell, the group would then add vocalist Layne Staley, along with drummer Sean Kinney and bassist Mike Starr. The group actually took its name from a previous band that had been led by Staley, which ironically was called Alice N' Chains. Although Alice in Chains is often identified with the grunge movement, their music has been described as oriented towards heavy metal, even though they still had elements of the former. Also unlike most of their peer's pre-Nirvana mania, the group had signed to a major label prior to their first album with Columbia Records in 1989.

After the success of *Facelift*, the group began in 1992 by releasing an EP called *SAP*. Although only an EP with 5 songs (one hidden), the album produced the hit single "Got Me Wrong," which would later feature prominently on the soundtrack for the movie Clerks, that would be released in October 1994, almost three years later. The band would then spend the early part of the year writing and recording material for their upcoming album, an LP that would be named *Dirt*. The album was very dark and dealt with traditional grunge themes such as drug addiction, loneliness, and anger, etc. One song, "Rooster," would be about Cantrell's father's experience in Vietnam. Unlike Pearl Jam and Nirvana, Alice in Chains' live act was split between Staley and Cantrell. Both men would sing, but it was Cantrell who wrote most of the lyrics and guitar parts. The vocal pairing of Cantrell and Staley, though, was seamless, like John Lennon and Paul McCartney. Still, Staley's stage presence was every bit as powerful as Vedder's or Cobain's, with his intense focus and, at times, howling vocals. The *Sap* and later *Jar of Flies* EPs would show a more melodic side of the band's songwriting, but none of this would be present on the upcoming *Dirt*.

Released on September 29, 1992, *Dirt* would prove to be every bit of a commercial and critical success as *Nevermind* or *Ten*. The album would spawn five hit singles: "Them Bones", "Down in a Hole," "Rooster,"

"Angry Chair," and "Would?" and would go platinum by the end of the year and 5x times as of August 2022. (riaa.com/platinum and gold) *Dirt* was also significant in the sense that it showed that there was a market for grunge/metal hybrids and that overtly dark-themed music also had a national audience. Although not as commercially successful as Alice In Chains (as of 1992), Soundgarden had also fused grunge and metal on *Badmotorfinger,* which in many ways is just as heavy as *Dirt.* The grunge moniker would also be applied to acts that could be considered derivative or just simply jumping on the bandwagon, as Cobain had accused Pearl Jam of doing in 1992.

Speaking of Soundgarden, for many years, they had been considered the premier band of the "Seattle sound". Having been formed in 1984, they had been around longer than most other bands in the grunge era. Singer and guitarist Chris Cornell's high-pitched, wraith-like shrieks were on a completely different level than most other singers of the era. One only has to listen to "Slaves and Bulldozers" on *Badmotorfinger* to truly understand this. Soundgarden was dynamic, though at times they were just plain heavy and louder than love. Composed of Cornell on lead vocals and rhythm guitar, the group also consisted of Matt Cameron on drums, Kim Thayil on lead guitar, and Ben Shepard on bass, replacing co-founder Hiro Yamamoto. As with Alice in Chains, Soundgarden's style was originally more metal/rock oriented, and its sound at times was just plain heavy and loud. As mentioned previously, the group had released two EPs and two LPs by the time they broke into the mainstream when *Badmotorfinger* was released on October 8, 1991. Singles such as "Rusty Cage" and "Outshined" would be successful and introduce the band's sound to a national audience. Although largely overshadowed by *Nevermind* at the time, the album would go on to achieve platinum status and would greatly increase the band's visibility. This, in turn, set them up for the runaway success of their next album, *Superunknown,* released in March 1994.

Of particular significance was the funk/rock/rap band The Red Hot Chili Peppers (RHCP). The band's massively successful and major label debut, *Blood Sugar Sex Magik,* was released on September 24, 1991, the same day as Nirvana's *Nevermind.* The band had been around since 1983, had been through many line-up changes, and was based out of L.A. The seminal lineup at the time of *Blood Sugar Sex Magik* consisted of frontman vocalist Anthony Kiedis, bassist Michael Peter Balzary (best known as Flea), drummer Chad Smith, and the brilliant, if somewhat mercurial, John Frusciante. Kiedis and Flea had formed the band and had seen its sound evolve seismically over the years. From its funk and joke-infused beginnings on their self-titled debut album in 1984, to the loud distortion, riffs, and overpowering assault of *Mothers Milk* in 1989, it had been a long journey for the band. Tragedy had struck when founding member and guitarist Hillel Slovak overdosed on heroin in June 1988. Kiedis would also struggle with the torment of addiction.

The stage act of RHCP was extremely intense and driven by hard funk/rap and rock in what was at the time a very unusual fusion. At times, they were flamboyant, zanny, and over the top (tube socks). Kiedis, in particular, was a very prolific performer and charismatic frontman. What made the group so unusual was its seeming obsession with sexual innuendos, sex, love, and women etc. However, by the time of *Blood Sugar Sex Magik*, the group had undergone a metamorphosis of sorts, and their songwriting had grown more reflective, melodic, and at times somber. The song "Under the Bridge", which details Kiedis's struggle with heroin addiction, reflects this shift. It is a melodic and introspective song that starts slowly and builds to a crescendo chorus underscored by the image of Kiedis running away from a nuclear explosion at the end of the music video. The song "Breaking the Girl" would continue this melodic trend, incorporating a mellotron to tell the story of a troubled relationship between Kiedis and an ex-girlfriend. The lead single "Give It Away" shows the group indulging its funk/rap origins. All these singles would be released throughout 1992 to great acclaim and help drive Blood Sugar Sex Magik to triple platinum sales within one year of its release. (riaa.com/gold-platinum) The RHCP may not have sounded, let alone dressed as grunge, but there is no denying that they were certainly alternative and influenced many grunge acts, and that they too were part of the grunge/alternative tidal wave that swept the music industry in 1992.

One major group that got stuck with the label of being derivative (unfairly or not) was Stone Temple Pilots (STP), who had massive commercial success with their debut album, *Core*, which was released on September 29, 1992, ironically the same day as *Dirt*. The band consisted of frontman and vocalist Scott Wieland, drummer Eric Cratz, and the DeLeo brothers, Dean on guitar and Robert on bass. That the group hailed from San Diego and not Seattle was already a knock against them with some people in the music world. Initially, STP was considered a knock-off of Pearl Jam, and Wieland was dismissed as an Eddie Vedder wannabe. A comparison that no doubt irritated Vedder. STP's sound was more rock-oriented than grunge, although it contained elements of the latter. Yet the group would soon find multi-platinum success and heavy rotation on MTV like their peers.

The group's live dynamic was very much centered around Weiland, who was known for his flamboyant and somewhat over-the-top stage performances with shades of Mick Jagger, the world-famous lead singer for the Rolling Stones. At times, he would sing into a microphone via a megaphone, particularly during performances of the song "Crackerman". Sadly, Weiland would struggle with the same demons of addiction to heroin that befell many of his peers, ultimately losing the battle when he died of an accidental overdose of various substances in December 2015. Songs such as "Creep" with lyrics, "Feeling uninspired, think I'll start a fire," and "I'm half the man I used to be" did speak to the angst often associated with grunge. Other songs such as "Sex Type Thing" dealt with the unpleasant subject of date rape and sexual assault. As will be discussed shortly, the music video for the song was quite controversial. One of the biggest hits off the album "Plush" was inspired by the kidnapping of a girl in the 1990s (a theme already echoed by the Nirvana Song "Polly"), and its accompanying video received heavy rotation on MTV.

Aside from music, there was also a political element to the grunge genre. Nirvana and Pearl Jam had both been outspoken in their support for pro-choice politics and had played several benefit concerts against censorship and in support of abortion and gay rights. At the same time that grunge was gaining in popularity in the Pacific NW, a subculture known as Riot Grrrl emerged from the same environs in Olympia, WA. Riot Grrrl was a feminist-based movement that incorporated not only punk and grunge- based bands but also politics, art, and women's issues specifically. Though the marketing of grunge had a decidedly male voice, feminism and inclusivity were central to the grunge ethos. Women artists, like Tori Amos, Liz Phair, and PJ Harvey, were major figures in the movement, loved, respected, and celebrated by their male peers. Toby Vail, also a central figure in the movement, founded the group Bikini Kill. Vail also dated Kurt Cobain briefly in 1990 and was allegedly the inspiration for the song "Drain You," which appears on *Nevermind*.

One group that had a big influence on the grunge scene was the LA-based all-female group L7. Formed in 1985 by Donita Sparks and Suzi Gardner, the group's second album, *Smell The Magic* (1990), was actually released on Sub-Pop. At times associated with the Riot Grrrl scene, the band also was the opening act on many occasions for Alice In Chains, Nirvana, Pearl Jam, and many other Seattle bands. In April 1992, they had their most commercially successful album with Bricks Are Heavy. Perhaps the most famous, or infamous, female grunge band was Hole. Led by Kurt Cobain's soon-to-be wife, Country Love, the group released their first album, *Pretty on the Inside*, in September 1991. The album was well received, particularly in the UK. Love's explosive lyrics and at times volatile personality went a long way towards increasing the group's profile as well as gaining her future husband's attention.

It cannot be overstated the role that MTV had in helping grunge bands further their careers and give them greater visibility both culturally and commercially. As stated earlier, several bands had already made music videos considered to be alternative in nature, such as Alice In Chains with "Man in the Box" and Jane's Addiction with "Been Caught Stealing" respectively. When the video for Nirvana's "Smells Like Teen Spirit" was released on MTV's 120 Minutes in late September 1991, it did not initially receive regular airtime. It would take MTV executive Amy Finnerty to push for a heavier rotation. Even went so far as to stake her job and reputation on the video's potential to be successful. (Cross, 2019, p.205) As *Nevermind* started to sell more and more throughout the fall, the video started to be played on a regular basis during the day. In many ways, it seems obvious as to why the video had the impact that it had, as the theme of the video is relatively simple. Set in a mock high school pep rally, it shows the band playing with their usual quiet then loud formula while at the same time the audience of restless teens grows increasingly unruly. It then eventually ends with them all forming one giant mosh pit while the band does their characteristic instrument-smashing set against the background of a growing fire. The message is a seismically significant one. "Here We Are Now Entertain Us" channels the unfocused angst of youth (mainly Generation X) into a memorable and powerful outlet. All the successful elements of a song combine into it and are amplified tenfold. Aggressive and catchy with loud guitars yet possessing an almost surgical pop sensibility to give it the hook. Just like The Beatles' "I Want to Hold Your Hand" almost 30 years earlier, Teen Spirit does not have to be explained; it is immediately understood universally. However, the Beatles did not have MTV in 1964. Nirvana in 1991-92 did. In spades.

In March 1992, Nirvana would release their second single off *Nevermind*, "Come As You Are," accompanied also with a music video. The video is set in a building-like structure with water constantly flowing down a set of stairs. A dog with a neck cone is shown slowly descending the steps and meandering about. The band is then shown playing behind a waterfall-like stream with their instruments and Cobain singing. They are seemingly concealed, and their faces are not shown directly while Cobain swings back and forth on a chandelier. As the song progresses, images of a revolver floating in water and sperm cells swimming about are also shown. The imagery, along with the lyrics of the song , combine to make a powerfully suggestive scene. It is an enormous credit to Cobain's songwriting skills that one can interpret his lyrics in a number of ways. Although more contemplative and less angst- driven than Teen Spirit, the song still possesses deep meaning and can instill a variety of emotions in the listener. The single and the music video also proved to be a major success.

Most songs that appeal to young listeners often speak of the common themes of love, relationships, and breakups, etc. Styles and genres may change, but youth and its experiences will buy and large always be the same. Idealistic and restless regardless of what time period they are living in. But there are times when a movie, book, song, etc. will tap into both the common themes of youth and the times they are living in and resonate on a very deep level. Nirvana arrived on the scene during a historical crossroads. The Cold War was on the verge of ending, and with the threat of nuclear war over, there was no overwhelming concern of World War III. There was no draft to protest, no war to fight or avoid, and there was no large-scale protest movement. In fact, there was no large protest movement of any kind on the national scene. Apathy has been a word that has been frequently used to describe Generation X, yet that would be an unfair label to throw about in regard to them. Restlessness and alienation would be more appropriate terms and fit better with the atmosphere of the early 1990s. However, angst would probably be the best term to describe the plight of the generation. It is hard to put into words what makes a song so special that makes its appeal universal. With Teen Spirit, Nirvana tapped into that feeling.

Another music video that was equally compelling, powerful as well and controversial was Pearl Jam's "Jeremy". Whereas Teen Spirit focused on youthful rowdiness and restlessness, "Jeremy" portrays a subject matter much darker and one that sadly would become all too prevalent in the 1990s. The video's main theme revolves around a teenage boy named Jeremy who is neglected at home and bullied or ignored at school. Vedder has spoken many times about his upbringing, and in some ways, the video could be interpreted as an allegory for his own childhood. The video switches back and forth between the band playing and the daily ordeal of young Jeremy being played out in the home and at school. Striking is the acting of the boy playing Jeremy and Vedder's intense performance, particularly his body language. One does not have to be psychic to know that Vedder's words come from the heart and experience. The lyrics of the song were just as searing as the video. "Clearly I remember picking on the Boy", "Daddy didn't give attention to the fact that mommy didn't care", "King Jeremy the wicked, rules his world," and finally "Jeremy spoke in class today". Throughout the videos, the camera pans between Vedder's intense facial expressions, hand movements, and culminates in young Jeremy's suicide in class by a handgun. The final scenes show still images of stunned classmates and a collage of phrases (64 degrees, white affluent suburb, etc.) describing the incident. As intense as "Smells Like Teen Spirit" was, it did not portray violence, let alone the suicide of a youth. Issues such as bullying and child abuse had never before been portrayed with such graphic rawness as in the Video "Jeremy". It was not just music, but very loud and resounding social statements that were being made. As intense as "Smells Like Teen Spirit" was, it did not portray violence, let alone the suicide of a youth. Issues such as bullying and child abuse had never before been portrayed with such graphic rawness as in the Video "Jeremy". For as intense as "Smells Like Teen Spirit" is, its destructive catharsis is exuberant, a youthful celebration. "Jeremy" shows a darker side of teenage growing pains. By focusing on the dangers and harms of bullying and abuse, Pearl Jam made a very loud and resounding social statement: sometimes, the kids aren't alright.

The success and controversy surrounding "Jeremy" would be such that Pearl Jam would refuse to make any more music videos for another three albums and six years. After "Smells Like Teen Spirit" and "Jeremy," no one could doubt the power of grunge and alternative to make a powerful statement and speak on issues that resonated greatly with Generation X. Neither could anyone deny that the new grunge, or alternative, music was here to stay. Other alternative artists would go on to make videos that tackled plenty of unpleasant subjects and themes. Alice In Chains, whose multi-platinum album *Dirt,* which was released in September 1992, would make a video for the single "Would?" that addressed the heroin addiction of Andrew Wood that eventually led to his death. Stone Temple Pilots, whose debut album *Core* was also a massive

1992

success, made a video for the first single "Sex Type Thing" that addressed date rape and received heavy rotation on MTV. Soundgarden's music video for the song "Jesus Christ Pose" off their breakout album *Badmotorfinger* would feature disturbing images portraying the crucifixion of Christ and would be pulled from rotation after several complaints from viewers perceiving it as anti-Christian. Nevertheless, the dam had burst, and there was no going back.

The lasting legacy of the grunge movement in pop culture was a concrete yet brief period in music history. The amount of time that elapsed from the release of Nirvana's *Nevermind* in September 1991 to Kurt Cobain's suicide in April 1994 was a period of only 2 ½ years. Yet during that time, mainstream music changed and evolved at a breakneck pace not seen since then. Since the grunge movement lost its cutting-edge relevance in the mid-1990s, it could be argued that there have not been any new genres of rock music or any type of music that has galvanized a generation or had a lasting cultural impact on a similar scale. Since grunge lost its cutting-edge relevance, it could be argued that there hasn't been another new genre of music, rock or otherwise, that has galvanized a generation on a similar scale. From the 1960 s up until the grunge movement, one could point to a specific style of music and how it was a product of its time. Psychedelic from the late 60's, disco and hard rock from the 70's, hair and heavy metal from the 80's, and finally grunge in the early to 90's. Sub-genres such as Techno and Nu Metal did gain some traction from the 2000 s onward. Yet it is safe to say that there is little difference in the lyrical content and sound of a Brittney Spears song from the late 1990s to a Taylor Swift one in the 2010 s or today. Compelling figures such as Amy Winehouse and Adele Atkins did emerge in the 2000's and while both wrote and sang great music, neither of them could be said to have represented a generation or changed the music industry on a universal scale.

The year 1992 saw Kurt Loder of MTV News state punk alternative grunge dragged, "kicking and screaming into the mainstream of music." It saw rock'n roll reborn anew and storm the charts, radio stations, major label companies, and most importantly, the hearts and souls of the youth of Generation X. It saw musicians dressed in flannel shirts and jeans full of holes spread their message of angst, frustration and rebellion on a national and worldwide scale. It was, as all truly great music and movements, from the garage and from the heart. In stark contrast to rock music of the past, it tackled subjects such as drug addiction, abuse, bullying, hopelessness, date rape and suicide. Most importantly, it told young people they were not alone and gave voice to their concerns and fears. It also gave them hope. One only has to look at the events that occurred on April 10, 1994, when thousands of grief-stricken fans of all ages converged on the International Fountain in Seattle to hear the now-widowed Courtney Love read excerpts of Cobain's suicide note. Statements were also made by Krist Novoselic, and grief counselors were also on hand to give advice and guidance while segments from their unplugged show, less than 5 months prior, were played repeatedly. Not since the plane carrying Buddy Holly, Ritchie Valens, and The Big Bopper went down had music suffered such a loss. Yet, the survivors gathered to carry on. At one point, the crowd stormed the fountain itself, leaving a compelling image of rebellious and angry youth. It was as if the crowd was epitomizing the very spirit of grunge and showing firsthand how it conveyed such deep resonance and feeling, and above all, posing the simple challenge, "Here we are now, entertain us."

1992

Pearl Jam frontman Eddie Vedder in his trademark helmet. Like Cobain, he did not revel in fame, yet he was initially suspect in his eyes.

Pearl Jam's performances were intense and emotional affairs that often involved Vedder climbing up on the stage rigging at great risk to himself.

Kurt Cobain was never comfortable in his unsolicited role as spokesman for a generation. Drug addiction and the pressures of fame would eventually consume him. Still, in 1992, Nirvana rewrote the musical landscape forever.

In 1992, the world became familiar with Nirvana's energetic, loud, and frequently destructive concerts. Here, the band gives arguably its greatest performance on August 30, 1992, at the Reading Festival in England.

CHAPTER 4

Bosnia and Somalia: Peacekeeping Missions and The UN Post-Cold War

For over forty years, a corner of Southeastern Europe known as the Balkans had been held together by a Communist dictator by the name of Josip Broz Tito, also known colloquially as Tito, who was the leader of Yugoslavia. Although a Communist, Tito gained notoriety by defying the Soviet Union and escaping the domination of the Iron Curtain during the Cold War. His charisma and adept political skills all combined to make him the unique leader he was, and helped keep him in power for over four decades. His death in 1980, although before the end of the Cold War and more than a decade before the Bosnian one, did signal the beginning of the disintegration of the former Yugoslavia and the eventual slide into the ethnic cleansing that came to pass throughout the 1990 s. What came to be known as the Bosnian War lasted from 1992-1995 and not only changed the region but also altered the dynamic of how force was used on the international stage.

The limits of force and how the nations of Europe, the United States, and even the world would respond to such tragedies would have far-reaching consequences. The aforementioned United States, along with most of the nations of Europe, with all its power and influence, and as the only superpower on the global stage after the collapse of the Soviet Union, would struggle to find a way to respond to the horrors that the conflict would produce. European allies would struggle to mount an effective response, and the United States would hesitate to become deeply involved. Europe would revisit the horrors of World War II with the mass expulsions of people based on their race or religion, the wanton slaughter of Muslims, Croatians, and Bosnian Serbs on a scale unimaginable for a people who until the war had lived side by side as neighbors, friends, and even husband and wife. Terms such as "Ethnic Cleansing" along with "Genocide" began being used regularly to describe the bloodshed. Where there had been an ethic of tolerance and peaceful co-existence, there was now primal hatred and vicious fighting. The Balkans had become bathed in blood.

To understand the Balkans and its history, culture, passions, and hatreds requires a great deal of study, as the region is so complex. The region comprises one of the most intense and compact makeups of religions, nationalities, languages, and ever-shifting borders on the planet. Due to these factors, intrigue, double-dealing, ultra-nationalism, and war have sadly always been a way of life for the region. The modern-day Balkans comprises the countries of Albania, Bosnia–Herzegovina, Bulgaria, Croatia, Greece, Kosovo, Macedonia, Montenegro, Romania, Serbia, and Turkey. A majority of the countries listed have seen their borders change as often as a conflict has broken out (which has been quite often). The Balkans have also often been used as a series of chess pieces by history's great powers in what has been called "The Great Game" of history. To recount the entire history of the region and the empires that have occupied and been driven out of it would take too long and is another subject entirely. What will be focused on is the Bosnian War and the events immediately preceding and succeeding it.

Yugoslavia was a nation that came into being from a World War and, upon its dissolution as a nation-state entity, saw its former republics embroiled in a bloody war amongst each other. Having been officially formed in 1918 as the Kingdom of Yugoslavia, the country provided a multi-ethnic and religious state for the South Slavs. The Kingdom was composed of six republics: Macedonia, Montenegro, Slovenia, Croatia, Bosnia/Herzegovina, and Serbia. During WWII, the country was invaded in April 1941, endured a brutal occupation by Nazi Germany and resisted with a guerilla campaign via what became known as the Yugoslav Partisans. The Partisans waged an effective and disruptive campaign against the Germans until the end of the war in 1945, when they were driven out of Yugoslavia. The person who led this guerrilla army was a man by the name of Josip Broz Tito. Tito, as he was simply referred to, was many things from a Communist revolutionary, guerrilla partisan, modernizer, and liberator, viewed reverently by Yugoslavians and others around the world. However, his greatest legacy would arguably be that for four decades he presided over a country whose people, despite their many nationalities, languages, and religious beliefs, lived in relative peace with one another. None of these changes the fact that Tito was authoritarian and used his cult of personality to great effect throughout his long rule to keep the peace.

Shortly after WWII, Tito's partisans took power in November 1945 and set up a Communist government. The Kingdom now became a Communist Federal Republic with Tito as its head of state. The Federal Republic of Yugoslavia had one national army, and the capital was in

Belgrade, Serbia. Despite being a Communist country, under Tito's leadership, Yugoslavia managed to stay out of Cold War geopolitics, and Tito himself led what became known as the non-aligned movement after he brazenly defied Joseph Stalin of the U.S.S.R. during the late 1940 s. Throughout the Cold War, the country developed and modernized in many areas, and Yugoslavia saw its international standing and wealth increase. Despite all of this progress, ethnic tensions were always simmering beneath the surface, and as a result, Tito gave more autonomy to the republics, and the state was more decentralized than other Communist countries. Then on May 4, 1980, Tito suddenly passed away. His death in and of itself was not the end of Yugoslavia, as the country had a series of Presidents who served one-year terms up until the end of 1991. However, it does seem safe to say that his death was the beginning of the end. Communism aside, it was Tito the man and Tito the legend's cult of personality that had held the Federal Republic together for forty-five years. Now he was gone, and it was only a matter of time before the country he founded also disappeared from the face of the Earth, but with disastrous consequences.

In November 1989, the much-hated Berlin Wall that divided the city and was a symbol of a divided Europe during the Cold War was forcefully taken down without any bloodshed. A year later, in 1990, one by one, the Warsaw Pact nations declared their independence from the U.S.S.R. Even the Republics of the Soviet Union, Ukraine, Belarus, Estonia, Latvia, and Lithuania began breaking away from the mother country and declaring their independence. Finally, on December 24, 1991, the Soviet Union was declared defunct, and the Russian Federation was proclaimed with Boris Yeltsin as its President. The Cold War was officially over, and new nations had arisen from the ashes of the Iron Curtain. With their newfound freedom in hand, the future seemed promising now that

Communism was finally gone. That hope spread to the soon-to-be defunct Federal Republic of Yugoslavia, where the six Republics, full of nationalism and ethnic pride, also sought to seize the moment and claim their own aspirations and independence.

The Republics are diverse in many aspects, from their language, religion, culture, and customs, etc. Croatia was Roman Catholic and spoke its namesake as its language. Serbia (Serbs) spoke Serbian and followed the doctrine of Eastern Orthodox Christianity, along with Montenegro. Bosnia-Herzegovina was predominantly Islamic (Bosniak) and spoke Bosnian, yet it also had a significant Serbian minority as well as a smaller number of Croatians (Croats). The southern Serbian province of Kosovo's population was majority ethnic Albanian, with a much smaller percentage of Serbs. The capital of Yugoslavia was located in Belgrade, which was in Serbia. Serbia had long been considered the dominant republic of Yugoslavia and, as such, fought against several of the Republics that sought to leave the Federation. Ethnic and religious differences aside, the Republics were also in the grip of a far more insidious force that combined with the former factors produced an extremely toxic mix. That force is nationalism. During Tito's long rule, nationalism was submerged under the ideology of both Communism and Tito's aforementioned cult of personality. The decade from Tito's death to the end of the Cold War saw the nationalistic pride of the Republics slowly start to seep to the forefront. In Serbia, this ultranationalist and xenophobic philosophy swept into power a man central to the events leading to the Bosnian War and beyond.

Slobodan Milosevic was born on August 20, 1941, during the German occupation of Yugoslavia. His father was a theologian, and his mother a devout Communist who later committed suicide. Milosevich earned a law degree from the University of Belgrade and began a career in politics through various posts within the Communist Party of Yugoslavia. He first gained national attention when he voiced support for the Serbs living in Kosovo who claimed they were being mistreated by the ethnic Albanian majority. Kosovo was a semi–autonomous province, and Milosevic advocated for greater ties to Serbia to keep them strong and dominant. In reality, Milosevic's vision was of a Pan-Serbian movement that would see Serbia extend its influence and power over the other Republics that had a significant number of Serbs living within them. In May 1989, Milosevic was elected President of Serbia. With the end of the Cold War rapidly approaching and the Federation weakening, Slovenia and Croatia both declared independence from Yugoslavia on June 25, 1991. After what became known as the "Ten Day War" with minimal casualties, Slovenia was granted independence under the Brioni Agreement. It is important to note that the fighting was not conducted by the Serbian Army per se but by what was known as the Yugoslav People's Army (JNA), which was controlled from Belgrade. Many Serbs simply felt that Slovenia was not worth the cost in blood and treasure, as there were very few ethnic Serbs living in the country as opposed to Croatia and Bosnia-Herzegovina. The first domino had fallen with little loss of life, but tragically, this would not be the case with Bosnia-Herzegovina. What became known as the Yugoslav Wars had begun.

As fighting continued in Croatia throughout the remainder of 1991 and into early 1992, Bosnia-Herzegovina (or simply Bosnia), Croatia's neighbor to the south, also began to debate independence from Yugoslavia. Unlike Croatia, Bosnia's ethnic Serb population was much larger, making the situation extremely volatile. In Croatia, the ethnic Serb enclaves were on the eastern border with Bosnia and the southern end of the eastern half of the country. At the start of the Croatian War of Independence, Serbs made up just over 12% of the population, whereas in Bosnia, they made up 31% to the Bosniaks 44%. (USHM.2013) Serbs were also a much larger political presence in Bosnia than they were in Croatia. In the fall of 1991, Bosnia formally began to debate whether to break away from Yugoslavia and Serbia. The deliberation within Bosnia's legislature was particularly acrimonious and full of vitriol. The President of Bosnia at the time was a man by the name of Alija Izetbegovic of the Party of Democratic Action (SDA). As a Bosnian Muslim, Izetbegovic strongly advocated for independence. Born on August 8, 1925, Izetbegovic was a philosopher, a Muslim, and a political dissident. From 1983 to 1988, he had served time in prison as a result of his activism on behalf of human and Muslim rights. After his release, he founded the SDA party and was elected President in a power-sharing agreement with the other groups of Bosnia in 1990. As relations between the Serbs, Bosniaks, and Croats began to fray, the agreement was dropped, and Izetbegovic would remain in office for the duration of the war.

Representing the Serbs in the debate was Radovan Karadzic, a Bosnian Serb and founder of the Serb Democratic Party (SDS). Karadzic was born on June 19, 1945, to a poor family from Montenegro and attended the University of Sarajevo to study psychiatry and start a career in medicine. During this time, he would make extra money by writing false psychological evaluations for a variety of reasons. In the 1980's Karadzic was arrested and spent eleven months in prison for fraud and embezzlement. He, along with several friends, founded the SDS in order to advocate for a Bosnia that would remain in Yugoslavia and be loyal to Serb interests. At one point during the debate Karadzic said that the Muslims did not understand the forces they were unleashing stating that, "Do not think that you will not lead Bosnia-Herzegovina into hell and do not think that you will not perhaps lead the Muslim people into annihilation, because the Muslims cannot defend themselves if there is a war." to which President Izetbegovic immediately retorted that, "His words and manners illustrate why others refuse to stay in this Yugoslavia. Nobody else wants the kind of Yugoslavia that Mr. Karadzic wants anymore. Nobody except perhaps the Serbs." (Little & Silber. 1995. p. 237) From February 29-March 1, 1992, Bosnians finally voted on whether or not to remain part of Yugoslavia. In a result that was completely boycotted by the Serbs, Bosnia voted to leave the Federal Republic of Yugoslavia with almost 99.7% of the vote. (Euronews, 2022) Karadzic had already formed what would be called the Republika of Srpska, with its capital in Banja Luka in northern Bosnia, two months prior, in addition to creating several Serb autonomous zones. For all intents and purposes, the Bosnian War had already begun.

Throughout March, the situation in Bosnia remained tense as both sides prepared for a confrontation. Izetbegovic appealed for calm and for the fact that for several decades, Serbs, Croats, and Bosnians had lived side by side peacefully. On March 1, a Bosniak Sniper opened fire at a Serb wedding in Sarajevo, killing one person. Throughout the city, Serbs began erecting barricades, and snipers became rampant. At the same time, Serb and Bosniak militias began taking up positions throughout the city.

On the mountainous terrain outside of the city, Serbs began taking up positions and placing their artillery at strategic points. A meeting between Izetbegovic and Karadzic in a last-ditch effort to avoid war provided only a brief respite when both parties agreed to joint patrols throughout the city by both the Federal Army (JNA) and Bosniak militias. At the same time, Milosevic was reinforcing his proxy Karadzic via the Federal Army of Yugoslavia. On April 5, a massive peace demonstration in Sarajevo turned bloody when demonstrators massed outside the headquarters of Karadzic. Serb snipers fired into the crowd, killing six people and causing mass panic. Bosniak forces quickly managed to restore order and arrested the Serb snipers while Karadzic fled to Serb-controlled territory just outside the city. On April 6, 1992, Bosnia's independence was formally recognized by the International Community. Shortly thereafter, the Serbs started to take control of cities in areas claimed by Republika Srpska and began systematically killing and expelling Bosniak Muslims who happened to live there. A taste of what was to come occurred on April 10, when Serb and JNA forces, having demanded that the Muslim occupants of the border town of Zvornik (who made up 60% of the population) leave, then stormed the city and began the process of "cleansing" via mass expulsions. One witness to this was ironically the United Nations High Commissioner for Refugees (Jose Maria Mendiluce), who, upon passing through Zvornik, remembered, "I could see trucks full of dead bodies. I could see militiamen taking more corpses of children, women, and old people from their houses and putting them on trucks. I saw at least four or five trucks full of corpses. When I arrived, the cleansing had been done. There were no people. No one on thestreets. It was all finished." (Little & Silber. 1995. p. 246) It was gruesome, horrific, and ugly. After all the rhetoric, posturing, and threats, the actual killing had begun. From the beginning, Karadzic was unapologetic in his vision of a Serb-dominated Bosnia, stating that Sarajevo would be the new capital of Republika Srpska even though the city was majority Muslim, with 51% to the Serbs 30%. (Zimmerman, 1996. p. 203) Charles Lane, a journalist for the New Republic, also provided eyewitness accounts of the ethnic cleansing in progress. While in Zvornik with a group of reporters, Lane saw three buses full of Muslim men proceed past who had "their beards shaved, their heads bowed and touching the seats in front of them, and their hands behind their necks." (Lane, 1996. p. 72)

As the fighting began, President Izetbegovic issued a public appeal for Bosnians of all ethnicities to defend the state against the Bosnian Serbs. A last-minute proposal by E.C. (European Community) special envoy Lord Carrington for a partitioning of the country into separate provinces for each ethnic group was rejected by Izetbegovic. The President was adamant that the territorial integrity of the country would remain intact and there would be only one Bosnia, having stated previously, "I would sacrifice peace for a sovereign Bosnia-Herzegovina, but for that peace in Bosnia-Herzegovina I would not sacrifice sovereignty." (Little & Silber. 1995. p.233) At the time, such a declaration and refusal to compromise would have seemed foolish on Izetbegovic's part, given the Bosnian Serbs' preponderance of military superiority in manpower, weapons, and outside support. Yet in hindsight, it seems safe to say that Izetbegovic's resolve and fortitude is what saved the country despite the bloodshed to come.

Radovan Karadzic's Serb army was practically under the control of Slobodan Milosevic in Serbia, from which it received many arms shipments and supplies, especially heavy artillery. Still, proxy or not, it was important for political purposes that Karadzic's Republika Srpska be seen as a separate entity. Thus, the Bosnian Serb Army (VRS) was created, which at the time was estimated to be between 90,000-100,000 men, at least 750 tanks, 1,000 APCs, 4,000 artillery pieces, 100 planes, and 50 helicopters. (Magas & Zanic, 2001. p. 155) The Serbs had long been planning an assault on Sarajevo, and mortar fire, along with shelling, soon commenced, followed by a ground attack in late April. At first, it seemed like the city would fall to the Serbs, and they would prevail as the Presidential building itself almost fell into their hands. Serb armor in particular was of great advantage at the onset of the assault. However, as the Serbs pushed deeper into the city, the Bosniaks began to rally. Sarajevo's narrow streets and alleyways, along with anti-tank weapons, began to halt the Serb advance. Of particular importance throughout the battle was the Bosniak Green Berets, a paramilitary force composed of former Yugoslav soldiers and Muslims loyal to the Bosnian state. By late April and into early May, Bosniak army units had begun to surround the Serb units in the city, themselves setting the stage for one of the most bizarre and unusual events in the history of warfare itself.

In early May, President Izetbegovic attended a peace conference in Lisbon, Portugal, and despite Sarajevo airport having been seized by JNA forces, insisted on returning to Bosnia on May 2. Landing at his own risk, Izetbegovic was immediately taken prisoner by JNA forces. For the Serbs, it seemed almost too good to be true. The enemy's head of state had unexpectedly

fallen into their hands. Despite the animosity between the belligerents, Izetbegovic was treated with respect and not abused. Izetbegovic was able to inform the Bosnian government of his capture by speaking to a woman who called the airport in order to find out if her son had made it safely out of the country. The woman then informed the Bosnian Presidency, who in turn began direct talks with the JNA in control at the airport. Ironically enough, the JNA was surrounded by Bosniak forces themselves, and they sought to use Izetbegovic as a sort of get-out-of-jail pass. Telephone conversations between Izetbegovic, his deputy, Ejup Ganic, were broadcast on Bosnian TV and local radio. The nation listened and saw firsthand how Izetbegovic remained calm and continued to project leadership during his captivity. To say the situation was strange would be a major understatement. Never before had the world seen a democratically elected head of state held prisoner within his own country, who had to negotiate and strike a deal for his own release.

An agreement was brokered by U.N. Commander and Canadian General Lewis MacKenzie by which Izetbegovic would be freed, and the JNA commander, Milutin Kukanjac, at the Federal army base where the President had been taken, would be allowed to leave the city and return to Serb lines. As the U.N. armored vehicle with Gen. MacKenzie, President Izetbegovic, and General. Kukanjac prepared to leave the base, the Federal Army demanded that their staff and equipment also be allowed to leave. Despite the sudden change in plans, Izetbegovic was prepared to use his personal authority to guarantee the whole convoy's safety. Unaware of the change in plans, Deputy President Ganic feared that he would be unable to keep total control of his forces, as many of them were paramilitary units.

As the convoy left the base and proceeded through Sarajevo, it was ambushed by Bosniak army units as well as paramilitary forces. As far as the Bosnian forces were aware, only the President and the JNA General had been granted safe passage, not his whole force. Izetbegovic emerged from the U.N. APC and, on the radio provided by one of his generals, attempted to order his forces to stand down and let the convoy proceed unmolested. Many of the Bosniak forces were angered by the carnage and destruction the Serb onslaught had wrought and wanted revenge. It was only with great difficulty that they finally backed down, and the convoy resumed its route. After twenty-four harrowing hours, Bosnia had its President back, and the JNA forces had left the city.

With the Serbs out of Sarajevo and very few left behind, the new Serb commander, Ratko Mladic, ordered the indiscriminate bombing and shelling of the city. No distinction was made between military targets and civilian ones as Gen. Mladic specifically ordered attacks on Muslim neighborhoods. The aim was to blatantly cause as much killing and destruction in the city as possible to "cleanse" it, so to speak. The siege of Sarajevo would continue until the end of the war, almost four years later. In the meantime, life for those who chose to stay or were unable to leave turned literally into a living hell. Daily life consisted of trying to avoid sniper and shell fire as well as dealing with the lack of water and electricity, which had been cut off in the city. Author and journalist Joe Sacco wrote a graphic novel called The Fixer (2003), which tells the story of a journalist (Sacco himself) who befriends an ex-Bosniak paramilitary soldier simply named Neven who makes a living ferrying foreign journalists to the front lines of the war. The novel gives a vivid portrayal of life during the siege of Sarajevo by narrating the main character's association with several local paramilitary warlords who are instrumental in the defense of the city during the early days of the siege. Many of them became what Sacco terms "military pop idols" as they gained fame for their brutality, ruthlessness, and effectiveness. The novel helps one to understand the complexity of the war as Neven, a Bosnian Serb, chooses to fight for the Bosniaks, despite them never fully trusting him.

Throughout most of 1992, the Bosnian Army was not a fully coherent force under the singular command of the government, as the airport/convoy incident with Izetbegovic illustrated. The Green Berets are the foremost example. Yet the government badly needed all the help it could get in fighting the Serbian onslaught. These paramilitary units did not always (if not most of the time) act in a manner consistent with the laws of warfare, and they even mistreated the Bosnian Muslims they were supposedly fighting on behalf of. Many of the paramilitary leaders had either criminal backgrounds or showed signs of mental illness. Stories of citizens being conscripted to dig trenches, ditches, and being forced out of their homes by the militias are portrayed as commonplace. Even more disturbing is the portrayal of the kidnapping and murder of a Bosnian Serb soldier loyal to Bosnia by his own side, demonstrating that the line between paramilitary force and criminal gang could be a very blurry one. Initially, such excesses were dismissed as being commonplace in war as the need for the paramilitary militias outweighed whatever problems that came with their "services".

As the war progressed, efforts were made to integrate these forces within the main Bosnian Army with mixed results. The case of one of these "Military Pop Idols" , Jusuf "Juka" Prazina, showed that some of these men were simply incapable of being team players or taking orders. Juka and his forces had played a significant role in the defense of Sarajevo, and he had been given command of a Special Forces unit as a reward. He then showed himself unable to get along with the Bosnian high command and proved to be a disruptive force at strategy meetings, prompting his expulsion from the country. In the fall of 1992, he reappeared in Bosnia and took control of an army base on Mt. Igman just outside of Sarajevo, which was the only land route in and out of the city, where he began extorting traffic going both ways. After being evicted from Mt. Igman by the Bosnian army, he and a few followers joined with Bosnian Croats and fought against his own countrymen and Muslims at Mostar in May 1993. After once again fleeing the country, his body was discovered in a ditch near Liege, Belgium, in December 1993 with two gunshot wounds to the head. His murder was never solved. These graphic novels not only provide great insight into the siege of Sarajevo, but they also remind us that it is important to remember that not all atrocities and war crimes were committed by Serbs alone.

As the story progresses, Sacco begins to have doubts about the credibility of Neven's stories. Is he simply embellishing? Or is he a pathological, if charismatic liar? After receiving confirmation that Neven did indeed serve in the war and bravely, he concludes that the answer may lie somewhere in between. Although it is never stated whether the main character is real or not, the local warlords described the conditions in the city, as well as what its citizens endured for four years very much is. Another story by Sacco tells the story of a young man, half Serb and half Muslim named Soba, who upon joining the Bosniaks at the beginning of the siege, sets and disarms mines at the front lines. Since the fighting is happening outside of Sarajevo itself, he does not really leave home. Hence, he enters civilian life every time he is off duty, albeit in a warzone itself. His story illustrates the understandable effort by those in the city to have some sort of normal life during the siege by going out to dance clubs and outdoor festivals, etc.

At first, the international community was slow to respond to the Bosnian War. This was in part due to its complicated nature. Although the world could see clearly the atrocities committed by Serbian forces and few doubted that they were real, Serbia and the disintegrating Yugoslavia did not pose a threat to the vital interests of the major powers of the Western world. These being mainly the United States, Canada, and the countries of the European Community (EC,) a predecessor to the current European Union (EU). Unlike Kuwait in the Persian Gulf, the conflict did not threaten global oil supplies. In many quarters, the conflict was seen simply as a civil war, albeit a very ugly one. Still, it was not lost on Europe that it was in Serbia almost eighty years before that a Serb nationalist had started the chain of events that led to World War I by the assassination of the Archduke Franz Ferdinand of Austria. The situation would need to be closely monitored.

Bosnia-Herzegovina became a member of the United Nations on May 22, 1992, following a formal appeal for outside intervention. This was followed by a demand from the Security Council that the JNA and all paramilitary forces from Serbia and Croatia leave Bosnia, which was simply ignored. (Magas& Zanic, 2001. p.157) By this time, an international relief force called United Nations Protection Force (UNPROFOR) had been established with General Lewis MacKenzie of Canada in command in Sarajevo. Formally established by U.N. Security Council Resolution #743 on February 21, 1992, UNPROFOR's mission was to deliver humanitarian supplies and medical relief for the Bosnians. Its mandate would also be to ensure the safety of those in established United Nations Protected Areas (UNPA), otherwise known as "safe zones," and ensure that the Sarajevo airport remained open. In what became known as Operation Provide Promise, the United Nations would conduct the longest ever humanitarian airlift from July 2, 1992 – January 9, 1996. This would prove vital in keeping aid flowing into the city and providing a link to the outside world. While the airport itself remained secure, the territory immediately around it was subjected to the usual sniper and mortar attacks that had become commonplace throughout the city. When Lord Carrington returned to the capital in an effort to start peace talks, his APC was hit by sniper fire.

Although UNPROFOR had military personnel and was authorized to use force if attacked, it was not a full-fledged combat force capable of offensive operations. Its efforts to distribute aid were frequently frustrated by Serb forces, who were less than cooperative. Compounding these issues was the fact that U.N. member nations were unwilling to commit any significant forces when Secretary General Boutros-Ghali requested 34,000 troops to protect the safe zones, and only 3,500 ended up being deployed. (Ching, 2009, p. 33) Most importantly, a No-Fly Zone was established over Muslim Bosnia for Serb military aircraft. The U.N. then imposed economic sanctions and an arms embargo in late May in the hope of stopping the flow of war materials into Serbia and the warzone. Sadly, it proved ineffective as Time Magazine reported in December that Bulgarian officials estimated at least 100,000 tons of crude oil and gasoline had made it into Serbia. (Time Editors, 1992, p.77)

One U.N. policy that had disastrous consequences for the Bosniaks in particular was what became known as the Arms Embargo. In the wake of the Croat Serb war in the summer of 1991, the United Nations Security

Council passed resolution #713, which forbade any weapons being sold or delivered to any of the former republics of Yugoslavia. The hope was that by stopping the flow of arms into the region that the bloodshed would be contained and not escalate past a certain point. Instead, it proved a blessing in disguise for Serbs and the VRS. As the seat of the former Yugoslavia (which now included just Serbia and Montenegro), Serbia inherited most, if not all, of the JNA's equipment and manpower. As mentioned previously, Bosnia did not have a coherent army formed when the conflict broke out in April, hence its reliance on the militias and "military pop idols". The U.N. Arms Embargo would eventually cause great friction between the U.S. and Europe in the coming years and at times threaten to split the alliance. (Meisler, 2013)

For all its good intentions, UNPROFOR was unable to stop the ethnic cleansing, the displacements and the rapes. In a scene reminiscent of the Holocaust in WWII, it could also not close the internment camps where mostly Bosniak men were sent once their villages, towns, and cities had been "cleansed" of non-Serbs. The Serbs denied that the men they had interred were being mistreated and, in a famous incident, literally exposed their own lies. A media company from the UK called British Independent Television News (ITN) was interviewing Radovan Karadzic and asked him point blank if there were human rights violations occurring. Karadzic invited the journalists to see for themselves, and two teams were dispatched to the camps of Omarska and Trnopolje. Upon arriving, the crews discovered famished and skeletal men languishing in captivity. (Ching, 2009, p. 28) Rape and sexual assault were also gruesome facts of life for Bosnian women and girls whose cities came under Serb occupation. As the Serbs occupied an area, they would inform the local city government that the town was now exclusively Serb, disarm the police, and deport, or kill in the case of the Srebrenica massacre, all of its male population. The Serbs would then literally have their pick of the local woman and often rape them on their whim. It was estimated that 50,000 Muslim Women and Girls were raped by Serb forces throughout the war. (Ching, 2009, p. 30) They would also be housed in camp-like settings, like their husbands, brothers, and sons, from whom they were separated. Many would never see their loved ones again. Such was the scale of the tragedy that on April 9, 1993, the grunge rock band Nirvana would play a benefit concert for the victims of rape during the war at the Cow Palace in San Francisco, CA. For a while, it seemed like Radovan Karadzic's prediction of "hell on Earth" and Muslim "extinction" would come to pass.

U.N. resolutions and UNPROFOR may have eased the suffering of the Bosnians in the beginning of the war, but as time went on and casualties mounted, it became obvious that only military force backed by political will can alter the situation on the ground. This seemed unlikely to happen anytime soon, as United States Secretary of State James A. Baker III specifically stated there "would be no unilateral use of United States force." His deputy Lawrence Eagleburger then echoed this by emphasizing that only humanitarian intervention would be forthcoming. Colin Powell, the highly respected Chairman of the Joint Chiefs, wrote in Foreign Affairs that the war in Bosnia simply did not meet his personal criteria for intervention in the conflict. (Zimmerman. 2003. p. 214-215) The UNPA's which were supposed to protect civilians, were only effective if both sides abided by and respected them. Still, they could not stop the slaughter as incidents such as the Sarajevo marketplace mortar attack in February 1994 and the Srebrenica massacre of July 1995 would grimly show. Throughout the summer and fall of 1992, the Serbs took over large swaths of Bosnia from both the Western and Eastern sides of the country. The Bosniaks controlled a central corridor spanning from Prud in the

North on the Hungarian border to Mostar in the Southwest along the Croatian border with besieged Sarajevo in the eastern central part of the corridor just outside of Serb-controlled territory. As complex and confusing as the conflict was for most outsiders to understand, it was about to take on an even more bizarre nature. In addition to the Serbs, the Bosnians were about to do battle with a neighbor who had been an ally and ironically, would be again.

As stated previously, the Bosnian War was but one component in the Yugoslav wars and was being waged simultaneously with the Croat Serb war. Who was fighting whom and who was on whose side seemed to constantly change. As both Bosnia and Croatia were fighting the Serbs in their respective countries, it seemed only natural that they would be allies, and in the beginning, they were. Like the Serbs in Bosnia, the Croats were a sizable minority comprising 17% of the population, concentrated mostly in southwestern and central Bosnia with outlying enclaves scattered throughout the country. (USHM, 2013) As was the case universally with the collapse of Yugoslavia, the Croats were enthralled with a fever- pitch nationalism and a desire to form a country based on their ethnic identity. However, within the Bosnian Croats, there were divisions as to whether they should seek to merge with Croatia proper or declare their own state from within Bosnia. In March 1991, Croatian President Franjo Tudman had even allegedly discussed with Serbian President Milosevic how to partition Bosnia between their respective countries. Everyone seemed to want the same thing: their own ethnic state. Everyone, except of course, Bosnian President Izetbegovic, who would not compromise on the territorial integrity of his new Republic.

Although the Bosnian Croats had proclaimed their own state, the Republic of Herzeg-Bosnia, on November 18, 1991, once the war started in April, both Croats and Bosniaks fought side by side and often in joint operations. One example of this collaboration was in the southwestern city of Mostar, where the Serbs had been repulsed and their siege of the city broken by Bosnian Croat forces (HVO) and Bosniaks in June 1992. In the same way the Bosnian Serbs received support from Serbia, the Bosnian Croats did as well from Zagreb, the capital of Croatia. Still, it was evident from the start that tensions existed within the alliance. The Bosniaks had their own agenda, as did the Bosnian Croats and the Croatians. Sometimes, the Bosnian Croats and Croatia proper did not agree on strategy. On September 14, 1992, the Constitutional Court of Bosnia declared the formation of Herzeg-Bosnia to be unconstitutional, which disheartened and angered many Bosnian Croats.

On October 18, 1992, the first open confrontation between the Bosniaks and Bosnian Croats occurred at a fuel depot in Novi Travnik. Other disputes followed over various issues such as who had responsibility for what sectors, towns, and who had authority/command over whom. Skirmishes played out in several cities and towns throughout Bosnia, with each side setting up roadblocks, fortifying their positions, and denying passage to the opposing side. In several towns and cities, the Bosnian Croats would forcibly expel Muslims and dissolve the local governments. Ironically in some ways, the Bosnian Croats were committing their own version of ethnic cleansing. One major factor putting the two sides at odds was the issue of religion, as the Bosniaks were Muslim and the Croatians Catholic. Making matters even more complicated was the fact that not all the territory controlled by one side, or either side, was fully contiguous. For example, central Bosnia was controlled mainly by the Bosniaks, yet they also controlled the northwest corner of the country. Likewise, the Bosnian Croats were concentrated mainly on the western edge of the country but had several enclaves on the eastern border with Serbia.

The rift between the Bosniaks, Bosnian Croats, and Croatians was seriously impacting their ability to fight against the Serbs effectively. As a result, on October 29, 1992, the town of Jace, located in the northern central areas controlled by the Bosniaks and Croats, fell to VRS forces. The fall of Jace was a disaster for both the Bosniaks and the Bosnian Croats as well as a great boon for the Republika Srpska. It was estimated that over 30,000 citizens were displaced by the defeat. The war within a war had taken on a life of its own. Two sides that were technically allies had started shooting at each other while still fighting a common enemy that was gaining ground. General Mladic gleefully proclaimed that he was happy to watch the two sides destroy each other so he could "push them both into the sea." If Bosnia-Herzegovina were to survive as a coherent nation state and political entity, some sort of solution would have to be found to bring the Bosniaks and Bosnian Croats to the negotiating table. As 1992 came to an end, just such a plan was proposed by U.N. Special Envoy and former U.S. Secretary of State Cyrus Vance and David Owen, former U.K. Member of Parliament and Secretary of State for Foreign and Commonwealth Affairs. What became known as the Vance-Owen Plan proposed that Bosnia-Herzegovina, which included territory held by the Republika Srpska, would be partitioned into ten separate and semi-autonomous Cantons: three Serb, three Bosniak, and three Bosnian Croat. The last Canton would make Sarajevo its own province. Although rejected by all three parties in early 1993, it would form the basis for what would become the Washington agreement which ended the Bosnian Croat War and established the Federation of Bosnia-Herzegovina on March 18, 1994.

As the year came to an end, the Bosnian War showed no signs of ending. The Bosnian Serbs had taken over 70% of Bosnian territory and expelled or imprisoned all non-Serbs in an orgy of ethnic cleansing, rape and murder. Sarajevo had been besieged and its inhabitants subjected to constant artillery and mortar attacks. They could not walk the streets without the fear of being shot by Serb or Bosniak snipers. Yet the Bosniaks had held on, rallied, and fought back courageously. For the time being, the Croats and Bosnians had fallen out and were now fighting one another for the same reason they were fighting the Serbs. Which ethnic group would rule which town, city, province, canton, etc. Only nine months ago, all three ethnic groups had lived side by side as neighbors, friends, even as family due to intermarriage. As harsh and authoritarian as Communist orthodoxy was, it had espoused a sense of brotherhood and coexistence espoused by Tito that transcended ethnicity and religion. Now all of that was gone in a seemingly unending vortex of carnage, hate, death, and destruction.

There was one forlorn hope for the situation improving when Serbia held its Presidential election on December 20, 1992. The man who stepped forward to challenge Milosevic in his re-election bid was Milan Panic, who had recently become President of the Federal Republic of Yugoslavia in July. A forceful advocate of democracy and a peaceful solution to the war, Milan was also a successful entrepreneur. It was hoped that if the election was fair, Panic might have a chance to topple Milosevic via the ballot box. Serbia's economy had suffered from high unemployment and inflation as a result of the war, and many people, particularly Serbian youth, were souring on it. The United States went so far as to threaten heavier sanctions if Milosevic won re-election and released a list of those it accused of war crimes, with Milosevic being the most prominent of those mentioned. In the end, it was not enough as Milosevic easily won reelection with 57% of the vote to Panic's 34%. (Wikipedia.org) International observers and Panic claimed that the election was fraudulent, and Milosevic benefited from control of the state-run media. However, all was not lost. Panic continued his advocacy for peace, and it was at his suggestion that U.S. President Bill Clinton convened a peace conference at Wright-Patterson Air Force base in Dayton, Ohio, where an end to the war would finally be negotiated in November 1995.

As the very first large-scale conflict faced by the world just months after the end of the Cold War, the international community had responded at best tepidly and in very small increments. Peace plans were proposed, no-fly zones set up, and arms embargoes put in place. Yet still, the killing continued unabated. In time, this would change as later events such as the Sarajevo mortar attack in February 1994 and the Srebrenica Massacre in July 1995 would finally galvanize NATO and the Western World into decisive action via the NATO bombing campaign in the summer of 1995 to bring about peace. Such events were sadly years away, and for many innocent victims of the war, they came too late. In 1992, with the Cold War having just ended, the world now had to figure out how to respond to events such as the Bosnian War. In time, they would learn that as important as negotiations, diplomacy, and humanitarian aid are, only military force in concert with all of these could alter the situation in a war zone. Perhaps the ultimate lesson of the events of Bosnia in 1992 is that hate and intolerance and the desire to segregate ourselves from the "other" are dark impulses that are just as much a part of the human character as our good ones are. Regardless of how civilized and enlightened we like to think of ourselves as being, we are all capable of reverting to the base savagery of the Bosnian War.

Just as Bosnia-Herzegovina was voting for independence in March 1992, a famine of near biblical proportions was unfolding in the war-torn East African nation of Somalia. Like the Bosnian War, it would also test the U.N.'s ability to respond effectively to humanitarian crises. The situation in the two countries in 1992 was similar in the sense that they both captured the world's sympathy for the amount of human suffering taking place and how the crisis should be handled. Yet there were significant differences. Yugoslavia had been a multi-ethnic state that had collapsed into open warfare when three of its republics tried to declare independence. Somalia was a unitary state that was, for the most part ethnically homogenous. The Somali famine had come about because of years of unending civil war between various factions, as well as the collapse of the central government after the ousting of the tyrannical regime of Mohamed Siad Barre. Barre's government was a military dictatorship with Marxist orientations, and like Tito of Yugoslavia, he espoused a strong brand of nationalism that helped keep tensions between different clans manageable. Also like Tito, Barre had ambitions to transform Somalia into a modern state, and his efforts met with some success. As the Cold War drew to a close, an increasing number of Somalians became dissatisfied with life under the dictatorship.

Many different militias had come together in order to overthrow Barre's government in early 1991, and once he was gone, a massive power vacuum occurred. Regular services provided by the government ceased functioning, and Somalia collapsed into anarchy. The rival factions then fought against each other for power over the country. After just over a year of fighting, a ceasefire was signed in March 1992 between the two most powerful warring factions led by the General. Mohammad Farah Aidid and General. Ali Mahdi Mohamed. Sadly, the ceasefire agreement was all but worthless, and the two sides practically never stopped fighting. The hopes and aspirations (or suffering for that matter) of millions of Somalis meant practically nothing to Aidid and Mohamed. All they cared about or ever would was their own power and how much control they could exert over the country for their own benefit. Humanitarian aid for them was a resource to be controlled and exploited rather than used to keep their fellow countrymen alive. The civil war had caused a great deal of destruction, and as a result, millions of people became refugees when their homes were destroyed. Although the U.N. had been active in Somalia in tandem with a number of relief organizations such as the Red Cross since early 1991, security had been very difficult to maintain, and it was impossible to keep the workers in the country for any length of time without them being endangered. With the situation on the ground rapidly deteriorating, the United Nations on April 24, 1992, created via resolution 751, United Nations Operations in Somalia (UNISOM) with the mission of monitoring the recently signed cease-fire and ensuring that humanitarian aid reached the general population.

From the start, UNISOM faced an uphill battle in carrying out its mission. To start with, the number of personnel for the mission was extremely limited. Less than 5,000 overall personnel were in the country at any one time. UNISOM had to contend with not only the major factions led by Gens. Aidid and Mohammed, but countless other militia groups were vying for power as well. With no one faction in control of the entire country, shipments of food and other supplies often had to cross over rival factions' territory to reach their destination. More often than not, they never made it at all. The shipments would either be extorted from U.N. personnel or outright stolen by not just the militias but any entity or person that had the means and will to do so. That the country was an unsafe environment to operate in should have been obvious long ago. Although efforts had initially been made to consult with all Somali tribal leaders, politicians, and various people of importance, it had not produced any sort of substantial cooperation with the U.N.'s efforts. Aid workers were often shot at, as well as ships unloading cargo at Mogadishu, which is Somalia's capital and a major battleground between the factions.

As dangerous as Bosnia was to operate in, the U.N. was at least operating hand in hand with a political entity (Bosnia-Herzegovina), albeit hardly a stable one. Somalia, by contrast, was a completely out-of-control vortex of chaos.

As the months passed, it was clear that UNISOM would not be able to carry out its mission until the security situation was brought under control. In early December, United States President George Bush approached the U.N. with the offer to lead a security force to help restore order, and his offer was accepted by U.N. Secretary General Boutros Boutros-Ghali. Unified Task Force (UNITAF), also known to Americans as Operation Restore Hope, was then set in motion. On the evening of December 4, 1992, President Bush went on national TV to announce the deployment and explain its objectives to the American people. Bush explained that only the United States had the capacity to intervene rapidly in such a distant country and also said that, "the United States alone cannot right the world's wrongs" but then added that, "American action is often necessary as a catalyst for broader involvement of the community of nations." The President then evoked images of docked aid ships crammed with supplies, unable to unload their cargo because of gangs controlling the streets, while Somalis starved just yards away. The speech ended with praise for the armed forces that they were doing "God's work" and a promise that they would have all the support they needed to achieve the mission, which would end once a secure environment had been achieved for the U.N. to perform its original mission.

For UNITAF, the United States would contribute a majority of the personnel for the mission, and most of the key command positions would also be held by American officers. Shortly thereafter, almost 30,000 American troops (mainly U.S. Marines and some Army components) began landing in Somalia and securing key areas such as ports and the airport. Ironically, the only reception they received was from the packs of journalists with cameras who knew when and where they were landing. In the weeks that followed, food and other supplies began to flow into the capital, and there was a sense that things were changing for the better.

However successful U.S. and allied troops may have been in providing security for the aid to be delivered, the situation could not last if rival militias and gangs were not disarmed and still roamed the country and cities at will. Among the Somalis, there was a feeling that the U.N. was playing favorites between the clans. In his book Black Hawk Down, Mark Bowden describes a member of the Habr Gidr clan, also the one General Aidid belongs to, expressing the sentiment that the Americans were only acting as agents for U.N. Secretary General Boutros Ghali, who was said to have a deep personal dislike of Gen. Aidid. (Bowden, 1999, p.71) Although welcomed at first, in time some Somalis would come to resent the U.N. and Americans as instances of excessive use of force and disruption of everyday life, as thousands of soldiers and equipment moved about them at all hours day and night. It should have been obvious to policy makers at the U.N., U.S. and elsewhere that it would only be a matter of time before they would be sucked into not only providing security and aid but also nation building both political and economic. The former would come to require direct confrontation with the militias and General Aidid in particular, as later events would show.

Ever since the Vietnam War, most Americans have been wary of undefined and open-ended use of the U.S. military in distant lands, particularly when there is no direct U.S. interest at stake. As he had with the Gulf War two years prior, President Bush had clearly defined what the role of United States forces and UNITAF would be. This was mainly to provide a secure environment for humanitarian aid workers to deliver food and medicine and operate. Once this objective was declared achieved, then

UNISOM II would come into being and take control. UNITAF had been an American-led operation specifically in name, and although UNISOM II would give operational control back to the U.N., the U.S. would still contribute the majority of personnel and equipment. UNISOM II would see the U.S. and its allies drawn further into warfare between the clans, culminating in the well-known events of Black Hawk Down. The October 3, 1993, raid on General Aidid's top lieutenants, although operationally successful, would prove to be the death knell of American involvement in Somalia. The gruesome images of dead American soldiers being dragged through the streets of Mogadishu no doubt angered and appalled the world. For Americans, it was fine to provide aid, but well-publicized deaths of U.S. servicemen were where the line would be drawn. In the wake of the hugely successful Gulf War, where minimum casualties were incurred, this was expected to be the new norm. Somalia permanently dispensed with such unrealistic expectations. War has been and always will be a deadly business that involves loss of lives. In the aftermath of the October 3 engagement in Mogadishu, President Bill Clinton ordered American forces to cease any offensive action against Aidid and his political party, the Somalia National Alliance (SNA). By early 1994, all U.S. forces had withdrawn from Somalia, and the year after UNISOM II's mission was concluded in March 1995. With the outside world gone, Somalians then returned to fighting each other, and the country descended back into anarchy.

The Bosnian War and the Somali famine both posed serious questions for the world community and the U.N. in particular in 1992. First and foremost, at what point does a nation state respond to a high-profile crisis that does not have any direct bearing on its own interests? Is a response measured and incremental, or all in from the beginning? What constitutes success? Finally, when do they leave?

In both Bosnia and Somalia, the United Nations had already been involved at a number of levels before either country made it into the headlines on a regular basis. The likelihood of severe sectarian violence in the former Yugoslavia was a possibility that all sides were well aware of, yet it was hoped that some sort of negotiated settlement could avoid bloodshed. Yugoslavia had been a modern nation state with infrastructure unlike Somalia. The United Nations had hoped to mitigate the level of carnage and risk to civilians with UNPROFOR in Bosnia, the same way they had hoped to mitigate starvation and famine in Somalia. In both situations, the U.N. learned a hard lesson. That being only the threat or use of military force can possibly hope to alter any calculus on the ground where the shooting is. Only with the leadership of the United States did the U.N. and NATO inch towards decisive military action against Serbia, and only after the Srebrenica massacre. In Somalia, after eight months of being unable to carry out its mission, UNISOM then gave way temporarily to UNITAF at the behest of President Bush. It was under UNITAF that order was temporarily restored, and the food was able to be delivered. It was in Dayton, Ohio, that the Bosnian War was finally ended in November 1995 at the behest of President Clinton.

The reality was obvious for all to see. The United States, as the only remaining superpower in the world had, for better or worse, become an indispensable nation in a post-Cold War world. For over forty years, the world had been divided geopolitically between two countries and their respective philosophies. All armed conflicts during that era had been viewed through the lens of the East-West dynamic, American vs. Soviet, Capitalism vs. Communism, etc. Any potential use of force had to be weighed against the probability that it might escalate and cause WWIII. This meant that regional conflicts such as Korea and Vietnam, where no direct interest of either party was at stake, American or Soviet, still had global implications.

In the wake of the Soviet Union's collapse in December 1991, conflicts such as Bosnia and Somalia were seen as simply regional in magnitude and however horrific, did not mandate the involvement of outside nations other than for altruistic humanitarian reasons. None of this is to say that the United Nations is inept on its own as an international organization of states. However, it is hard to ignore the reality that decisive action in a country torn by war or famine can only come about through the will not only to use military force, but to incur casualties and the political will to stay the course. This can be difficult when one pilot being shot down or one soldier being taken prisoner has the potential to change public opinion overnight, particularly in the age of smartphones and social media. Involvement may come about incrementally or wholesale, depending on the conditions of the conflict. However complicated and drawn out such interventions can be, there is also the danger of inaction or non-involvement, as the dark abyss of the Rwandan genocide in the summer of 1994 showed all too clearly.

Over the course of a 100-day period from April-July 1994, several hundreds of thousands of Tutsis, a minority tribe in Rwanda, were slaughtered by the majority Hutu. During this time, the U.N.'s small peacekeeping force was simply withdrawn, and no serious attempt was made to stop the slaughter. The United States, still licking its wounds from the Somalia intervention, had no desire to intervene in a conflict. Neither did the international community, as the gut-wrenching memoir of Canadian General Romeo Dallaire, Shake Hands with the Devil: The Failure of Humanity In Rwanda, brilliantly illustrates. Gen. Dallaire makes the very upsetting observation that the United States chose not to intervene because the estimated cost of $8,500 per day of jamming a radio station that played a role in inciting the genocide wasn't worth saving 8-10,000 Rwandans being killed daily. Even more disturbing is the rationale that jamming a country's airwaves violated its sovereignty which, while legally correct, meant nothing to the victims of the killings. (Dallaire. 2003. p. 375)

Going forward into the 1990s and beyond, the international community, more specifically NATO and the UN, would respond to many more conflicts, civil wars, and unrest, etc. Less than six months after the US had pulled all of its forces out of Somalia in March 1994, the country was forced to deal with a crisis much closer to its own shores. The Caribbean nation of Haiti has been in the hands of a military Junta since September 1991, when a military coup overthrew the democratically elected government of Jean Bertrand Aristide and installed military officer Raoul Cedras in power. Efforts to negotiate a return to democracy with Cedras proved futile, and thousands of Haitians fled the country to the United States, causing a humanitarian crisis.

By July 1994, the situation had reached a boiling point, and President Clinton, acting with the approval of the UN Security Council, assembled a coalition of various nations throughout the Caribbean, Central, and South America. By late September, the multinational task force was poised to invade, and Clinton even had the 82nd Airborne Division ready to deploy. Fortunately, at the last moment, Cedras backed down and surrendered power after some hard negotiating from former President Jimmy Carter, Ret. Joint Chiefs Chairman Colin Powell and Georgia Senator Sam Nunn convinced him his cause was hopeless. As with Somalia, the United States acted forcefully with the blessing of the UN, and Aristide was returned to office. American leadership, in concert with the UN and NATO (where applicable geographically), seemed to be the new template emerging for how the world responded to international crises.

The US, its allies, and NATO would not always have the blessing of the UN in future conflicts. In early 1999, war again broke out in the Balkans when Serbia, with Milosevic still in power, launched a campaign of ethnic cleansing against the ethnic Albanian majority in the semi-autonomous province of Kosovo. Unable to get a Security Council vote to back military intervention due to Russian and Chinese opposition, NATO launched a successful three-month air war on its own. In February-March 2003, President George W. Bush was also unable to get the Security Council to vote on a resolution to authorize the 2003 Iraq War on the grounds that Iraq had weapons of mass destruction and had not fully cooperated with previous UN resolutions demanding they disclose and disarm whatever stockpiles of WMD they allegedly possessed. Bush then led what he called a "coalition of the willing" and prosecuted the war with token help from other countries.

In March 2011, President Barack Obama would revive the template somewhat by joining a NATO-led air campaign against Libyan dictator Muammar Gaddafi, who was in the midst of a civil war against anti-government forces attempting to overthrow his long-standing regime. In a break from the recent past, Obama decided to leave the overall direction of the campaign to British and French forces and instead chose a policy of "leading from behind" as his approach for the intervention came to be known as. After eight months, Gaddafi was dead, and the regime gone making the intervention a success even though Libyans would face years of chaos and renewed civil war.

President Obama would have one surprising success overseas and not with the help of the U.N., but ironically an adversary. During the "Arab Spring" of early 2011, civil war broke out in Syria at roughly the same time as Libya. The president of Syria, Bashar al-Assad, had amassed a large stockpile of chemical weapons, and it was feared that he might use them on opposition forces and innocent civilians. President Obama had stated that the use of such weapons would be crossing a "red line," implying that military intervention from the US would be forthcoming. In August 2013, Assad carried out just such an attack with sarin gas, which killed 1,500 civilians. President Obama responded by stating that direct action would be taken against the Assad regime. Then, just as soon as he made the announcement, the President decided it was necessary to get congressional approval before acting. With the country's direct participation in the Iraq War having only ended not even two years ago and the U.S. still committed to Afghanistan, the American public was strongly opposed to any new foreign military intervention.

It seemed that Obama's red-line threat rang hollow and that he would be powerless to act unilaterally. A few weeks later, Secretary of State John Kerry stated offhandedly at a conference in London that the only way to avoid war in Syria was for Assad to give up his chemical arsenal, which seemed unlikely to say the least. A delegation of Syrians was meeting in Moscow with the Russian Minister of Foreign Affairs, Sergey Lavrov, while Kerry was in London. Lavrov had unintentionally taken Kerry's pronouncement as actual policy and saw a chance to act on it, as luck would have it. Obama chose to act on the initiative, and over the next few weeks, the US and Russia hammered out an agreement to dispose of all of Syria's stockpiles of chemical weapons, which were estimated to be more than 1,300 metric tons spread out over 45 sites. (Chollet, 2016) The destruction and removal of the weapons was then accomplished in short order. Given the ascendance of ISIS in Syria the following year, this unexpected disarmament would prove a godsend. Such a strange international deal helps to illustrate how unintended initiatives lead to unintended opportunities. It also shows how so-called "soft power", co-opting instead of coercing by diplomacy, can be truly effective on the world stage in a bilateral sense.

The year 1992 would show an international order that could not everywhere yet unfairly be expected to be. It would show a U.N. that was expected to decisively intervene in complex conflicts, reason with intractable belligerents that had centuries-old grievances and ease the suffering of those affected by these conflicts. Multi-literal peacekeeping missions became the new norm in a post-Cold War world. Its efforts did achieve results, even if only temporarily in the case of Somalia. Still, the U.N., when backed by proper support from its member states, has been able to make the effort and show that humanity does not fail, as Gen. Dallaire states. In the end, international organizations such as the U.N. and, more regionally, NATO can only be as effective as their member states want them to be.

1992

Architect of Genocide. General Ratko Mladic, commander of the ground forces of Republika Srpska. As a proxy of Serbian President Slobodan Milosevic, along with Radovan Karadzic, President of Republika Srpska, they were given ample arms and had a free hand to facilitate the ethnic cleansing that would become so familiar to the
rest of the world.

The siege of Sarajevo was a ghastly humanitarian nightmare marked by indiscriminate Serb shelling and countless civilian casualties. The siege would last four long years and only end in early 1996. The UNIS twin towers, a prominent symbol of the city, in downtown, were severely damaged during the siege.

Alijah Izetbegovic, President of the newly independent Republic of Bosnia-Herzegovina. His fortitude in the face of the Serbian onslaught galvanized the Republic and ensured its survival, but at great cost.

CHAPTER 5

Rodney King, Race & Society

Of the many transformative events to occur in 1992, social, cultural, political, musical, etc, it goes without saying that not all were peaceful and without bloodshed. One incident made clear that even almost three decades after the signing of the Civil Rights Act of 1964, deep racial divisions festered close to the surface of American society, ready to explode given the right spark. A man by the name of Rodney King and five LAPD officers would provide that spark and provoke the worst incidents of racial rioting seen in the United States since the Watts Riots of 1965. In little more than five days in April and May 1992, most of South-Central Los Angeles was burned to the ground and gutted by an angry Black population furious over an almost all White jury's acquittal of five white police officers caught on amateur videotape in the act of severely beating motorist Rodney King. Much like the George Floyd riots twenty-eight years later in 2020, the unrest surrounding the Rodney King beating would attain a symbolism and meaning that went far beyond the actual men themselves. Issues of policing, the U.S. criminal justice system, and various inequities throughout society would come front and center to the public eye.

It can be arguably stated that Rodney King had a very significant impact because it not only dealt with police brutality and American policing, but also civil governance and the criminal justice system as well. Many hard questions about racial relations and equity also came to the forefront. As with many events throughout history, it is important to understand past events that led up to the present ones. The Rodney King Riots of April 29- May 4, 1992, are no different.

Like much of the United States, Los Angeles has a long history of racial discrimination and bigotry. African Americans had begun to move westward in large numbers during the Second World War as industrial production rebounded from the Great Depression and job opportunities were plentiful. President Franklin D. Roosevelt had banned federal employment discrimination via executive order so that many black people could, ideally, be hired based on qualifications and evaluated according to their performance and ability. Once the war ended, many black families settled in South Central Los Angeles, particularly in Inglewood, Compton, and Watts. African Americans had hoped that their heroism and patriotism in the war would wipe away discrimination and give them the same opportunities as whites. Sadly, like their ancestors after the First World War and the Civil War before, they returned to a country whose social and racial attitudes had scarcely changed. Instead of Jim Crow, now it was restricted housing covenants that denied Black families their dream of home ownership in white neighborhoods. Even African Americans who were well established professionally faced an uphill battle to secure decent housing. One Robert Joseph Pershing Foster, a surgeon on the make who had fled his native Louisiana because he was unable to practice medicine, was told that when he was about to rent an apartment for his family in Los Angeles that the unit was no longer available despite Foster having ample funds. (Wilkerson. p. 282. 2010) It must be noted that although

African Americans bore the brunt of these covenants, other minorities were adversely impacted by them as well. By the 1940's Los Angeles was home to minorities from all over the world, especially Asians and Latinos.

Although Los Angeles continued to grow and prosper over the next two decades, tension was boiling beneath the surface, and it was only a matter of time before it exploded. That breaking point came in the form of a drunk driving arrest on August 11, 1965, when a young man named Marquette Frye was pulled over in the Watts neighborhood of Los Angeles and failed a sobriety test. Frye's irate mother quickly arrived on the scene and began to berate the officers involved in the arrest. Crowds from the surrounding houses also began to gather and harass the officers. From this point on, events rapidly escalated into an all-out riot in Watts and the surrounding area of South-Central Los Angeles. Over the next six days, it took over 16,000 National Guardsmen along with local law enforcement to quell the riot and restore order. Although civil protest and riots were commonplace throughout the 1960's what made the Watts riots different was the fact that the disturbances went beyond rioting and looting but involved actual urban combat with rioters engaged in running gun battles with the authorities. Astonishingly (at least to the White journalists and researchers conducting interviews and gathering data), most African Americans interviewed in the aftermath of the riots referred to them not as riots but as "rebellions". The amount of popular support the riots generated within the Black community makes this categorization plausible. According to the McCone Commission, it was estimated that 22,000 people took part in the riots while an estimated 50-60,000 people sympathized with and supported the rioters. (Williams. p.144. 1969) An even more ominous omen was that out of the 3,438 persons arrested, 1,164 had only minor infractions with the law, while 1,232 had no criminal record whatsoever. (Fogelston, p. 154, 1969) As the 1960s played out, Watts would hardly prove to be an isolated incident.

In the aftermath of the Watts riots, a California state commission was created under the leadership of ex-CIA director John McCone to investigate the disturbances. The main causes of the riots, as determined by the commission, were unsurprisingly poor housing, low income, and limited educational opportunities, just to name a few. All these factors were compounded by the fact that the residents of Watts were still unable to buy homes in safer neighborhoods (if they could afford them) due to restrictive covenants that banned them. An attempt to address this injustice had been made by California Assemblyman William Rumford, who authored what became known as the Rumford Fair Housing Act in 1963, which banned discrimination in real estate, housing, and rentals based on ethnicity, religion, and national origin. Although the Rumford Act became law, it was struck down in the 1964 general election by Proposition 14, which basically made it legal once again for landlords and real estate agents to discriminate as they pleased in who they decided to sell or rent to. Ironically, Proposition 14 itself would be struck down by the California State Supreme Court in 1966. What became known as "White flight" became a reality when large numbers of White families began leaving the cities and moving to the suburbs rather than have African Americans and other minorities as neighbors.

Over the next two decades, the relationship between the LAPD, the poor, and minority citizens did not improve. Throughout the turbulent 1960's as disorder and rioting became commonplace, policing became more aggressive and reactive. This approach carried over into the 1970s and 80s when gang violence and the crack cocaine epidemic exploded. In 1978, Daryl Gates became Chief of Police for Los Angeles. A career officer who had served since 1949, Gates implemented several new initiatives and programs within the department, such as D.A.R.E. (Drug Abuse Resistance Education) and C.R.A.S.H. (Community Resources Against Street Hoodlums). Gates was also instrumental in the creation of what became known as the first S.W. A.T. (Special Weapons and Tactics) teams in conjunction with LAPD Sergeant John Nelson in late 1965, after the Watts Riots had shown the difficulty regular patrol officers had in responding to urban street fighting. Street gangs also became a major issue in several neighborhoods, especially the Crips and the Bloods which were founded in 1969 and 1972 respectively.

In 1987, LAPD commenced Operation Hammer, an extremely aggressive anti-gang operation throughout the city. As officers flooded South Central and East L.A., large numbers of arrests and raids were conducted to discourage the gangs and crack down on drug dealings. Thousands of people were arrested without being charged, and officers, to frighten gangs and drug dealers, often trashed and destroyed the property that was being searched. One notorious raid, conducted on August 1, 1988, went a long way to foster animosity between the police and the Black community in South Central. Residents of Southwest L.A. had long complained to the police about the impunity with which drugs were sold in the neighborhood and how unsafe it was at night. The police decided to conduct a large-scale raid on two apartment complexes on the corner of 39th St. and Dalton Ave. During the raid, LAPD officers brazenly and deliberately destroyed the property of several residents as well as physically assaulted them. All the police were able to find was a minuscule amount of Marijuana (six oz.) and not even one ounce of cocaine. Even worse, the Red Cross had to provide aid to twenty-two people who became homeless because of the raid. (Mitchell, 2001)

Years of racial tension had been building between the races of Los Angeles for many years, with complaints from Black population of routine brutality and excessive force used by police officers. A routine tactic of submission that had been used by the LAPD was to employ a chokehold with a baton on suspects resisting arrest, many who happened to be Black. Throughout the 1980s of the eighteen suspects who died because of the chokehold, sixteen of them were Black. (Williams. p.121. 1993) Chief Gates defended this method by stating that African Americans were more susceptible to such tactics because their circulatory system was different from Whites and other races, which did not help matters at all.

Eventually, the use of the chokehold was banned by Chief Gates, which meant that officers now had to rely on the use of tasers or batons to gain control over a resistant suspect. Many at the LAPD police academy were at a loss as to how to train officers to take suspects into custody without the use of physical force likely to cause grave injuries to those resisting arrest, as the brutality of the Rodney King beating would show to all the world. Despite the strenuous protest of training personnel, no attempt was made to find an alternative to the use of the baton in place of the chokehold. As expected, use of the PR-24 baton caused almost as many injuries and complaints of excessive force as the chokehold. As a result, an astronomical increase in the amount of settlement money to victims occurred from $891,000 in 1980 to over $11 million in 1990. (Cannon, p. 105.1997) Still, Gates would try to push for a partial reinstatement of the chokehold for use only in non-lethal situations. To support this request, Gates argued that according to statistics from an eighteen-month period before the chokehold moratorium (May 12, 1982) that officers injured in use-of-force situations had increased 181%, and the number of suspects injured had increased by 395%. (Koon. p. 57. 1992) Despite these figures, his request to the Police Board (the panel that makes decisions regarding policies and procedures) was denied. Gates and Sgt. Koon would argue that politics killed the use of the chokehold, not practical concerns, and police personnel, along with those on the receiving end of the PR-24, would pay the price in the field. So great was Koon's faith in the chokehold he would later assert in regards to the Rodney King arrest, "All we would have had to do was to swarm him with a chokehold, and the entire episode would have been over in fifteen seconds. The video tape would have only captured a brief scuffle." (Koon. p.60-61.1992) Regardless of training standards and what can or cannot be done in an arrest, another major problem was not just simply law enforcement tactics in and of themselves but the quality of people being hired by LAPD. The starkest example of this would be one of the officers involved in the Rodney King incident itself.

Laurence Powell, the officer who was seen landing more baton strikes on King than any others in the video, was, like so many other police officers involved in issues of police brutality, a very problematic officer. Having been encouraged to pursue a career in law enforcement by his father, it was obvious to many of his fellow officers and others that Powell was simply not a good fit as a police officer. Interviews from numerous sources paint a picture of a man who was at times, crass, rude, and immature. After dealing with a domestic dispute involving a Black husband and wife, Powell later remarked that the episode was like "Gorillas in the Mist." Many female officers were quoted as saying that Powell was sexist and prone to making inappropriate remarks. Despite these personality traits, Powell also had many supporters over the years. Powell had graduated at the top of his class at the L.A. Police Academy, and one of his instructors felt that he had a bright future in law enforcement ahead of him.

Inner-city life for Black Americans had been dangerous long before the Rodney King riots. Urban blight combined with gang violence, drugs, and few opportunities for Black youth created an environment impossible to thrive in, let alone feel safe. In the late 1980s, a new music genre emerged to give a voice to its inhabitants. While Rap and Hip/Hop in 1992 was still a relatively new musical genre, it had changed a great deal since Sugar Hill Gang's "Rapper's Delight", considered the first Rap song, was released in 1978.

In the late 1980's groups such as Public Enemy and N.W.A (Niggaz with Attitudes) heralded the dawn of what became known as "Gangsta Rap". The lyrics of this genre were more violent, dark and explored themes such as teenage pregnancy, drug abuse, rape, life in the ghetto (or known more colloquially as the "hood") and in many cases, disrespect and hostility towards law enforcement. This was especially true in the case of the song "Cop Killer" by the L.A.-based thrash/metal group Body Count, of which prominent rapper Ice-T was the lyricist and writer. Released in 1992, the song was extremely controversial for its subject matter and lyrics which stated, "Die, die, die pig die. Fuck the police. I'm a cop killer, fuck police brutality." Both President Bush and Vice President Dan Quayle publicly condemned the song. Another artist who had a big impact that year was Dr. Dre, who released his debut album The Chronic on December 15, 1992. Although released at the end of the year, the album was in the process of being recorded when the verdict was announced and the ensuing riots. In addition to the usual songs depicting drugs and gang related violence, one chilling and compelling track, "The Day the Niggaz Took Over", vividly describes the climate in which the riots took place and the mindset of those who participated in it. Over the course of the song, one hears lyrics such as, "Cause I'ma cock my glock and pop til they all drop", "I said how many niggaz are ready to loot? Get myself an Uzi and my brother a nine" which depicts looting, arson and violence against police.

One artist in particular came to symbolize the genre before he, too was sadly struck down by gang violence. In November 1991, Tupac Shakur released his debut album 2Pacalypse Now. In the album, Shakur echo's familiar themes of life in the ghetto, such as teenage pregnancy on "Brenda's Got A Baby" and police brutality and harassment in "Trapped". Although born in New York City, Shakur, who was born Lesane Parish Crooks on June 16, 1971, would eventually make his way out to San Francisco and become a central figure in the West Coast Hip-Hop scene that fused rap and politics. Born to parents who were both members of the Black Panther Party, Shakur became politically aware at a young age to the reality of life in the ghetto and what his future would entail if he did not get out. Highly intelligent yet volatile, Shakur also showed interest in acting and poetry, from which he launched his rap career. Having made his professional debut with the group Digital Underground in 1990, Shakur already had a significant level of visibility within the genre. Shakur would also come to symbolize the East-West coast feud between prominent rappers throughout the 1990s. His songs gave voice not only to the reality of the ghetto, but the simmering tensions between black people and law enforcement. Given all the distrust and animosity between the LAPD and the Black community, it seemed only a matter of time before another incident would cause those tensions to explode.

Perhaps not since the Zapruder film, shot by Dallas dressmaker Abraham Zapruder, that captured the Assassination of President John F. Kennedy, has an amateur recording had such a profound and far-reaching impact. This is considering that even the Zapruder film did not cause rioting, loss of life, and widespread property destruction. On the night of March 3, 1991, a man by the name of Rodney Glen King was being pursued by law enforcement for driving at speeds of up to 115 miles per hour. California Highway Patrol Officers Timothy and Melanie Singer pursued and then arrested two passengers in his vehicle after King finally came to a stop outside of Hansen Dam Park and in the vicinity of the Lake View Terrace neighborhood. Five Police Officers from the LAPD then subsequently arrived on the scene. As Melanie Singer shouted at King to lay face down and submit to arrest, it became apparent to the officers on the scene that King was possibly under the influence of alcohol, drugs, or both. His behavior after exiting his vehicle was erratic and strange. King's face was glistening with sweat, and he was scantily dressed despite the cool temperatures of that evening. LAPD officers Sergeant Stacey Koon, officers Timothy Wind, Laurence Powell, Theodore Briseno, and Rolando Solano, then took over the arrest at the behest of Sgt. Koon, who was the ranking officer out of all those present. Sgt. Koon was an experienced officer with over fourteen years with an LAPD, and he had been in many tense and dangerous situations during his time in the force. In an action that he believed had saved King's life, Koon ordered all officers present to holster their firearms (Singer already had hers drawn on King initially). It was Koon who initially thought King was possibly on PCP, a drug that supposedly made one impervious to pain and gave them superhuman strength. This suspicion was confirmed when, in Koon's directions, officers Powell, Wind, Briseno, and Solano attempted to physically restrain King, take him into custody, and were literally tossed off with ease by him. Koon, then having unsuccessfully attempted to taser King, who still would not respond to verbal commands, watched as King rose to his feet and charged Officer Powell, who then struck him across the face with his PR-24 baton. Over the next eighty-two seconds, King was struck by both Powell and Wind with an estimated fifty-three baton strikes while also being kicked repeatedly by Wind. The situation, which had rapidly turned violent as King resisted arrest and was severely beaten, was also being filmed on a hand-held video recorder, unbeknownst to all involved, by a man named George Holliday.

Holliday lived in an apartment complex from which he was able to witness and videotape the beating from his second-story unit. The video shot by Mr. Holliday shows police repeatedly attacking King with their batons to subdue him. The portion of the video mostly shown to the public shows a prostrate King being struck repeatedly with multiple batons, mainly by Powell, but with Wind also making several swings in addition to kicking him. Briseno is seen momentarily trying to move Powell away from King before stepping out of the way before Powell starts swinging again. The King is seen trying to rise to his feet while being struck back down several times before finally being swarmed by a group of officers and taken into custody. Holiday immediately understood that what he had filmed was of great significance, but also a terrible injustice likely to shock and anger the public. It was highly unlikely that Holiday (or those being recorded) at that moment could truly grasp how massive the impact of his recording would become. Still, he resolved to try and make the tape public as soon as possible.

Just two weeks after the Rodney King arrest, another incident occurred that would further strain relations between African Americans and Koreans within L.A. On March 16, 1991, a thirteen-year-old girl named Latasha Harlins was walking home from a friend's house when she stopped at the Empire Liquor Store located on West 91st. St. and South Figueroa. Harlins entered the store and took a bottle of orange juice out of the cooler, partly placing it in her backpack. As Harlins walked towards the register, the woman behind the counter, Soon Ja Du, was convinced that she was trying to steal from the store.

Over many years, relations between Korean store owners and Black people had been poor and showed no signs of improving. Korean

Americans owned several convenience stores throughout Los Angeles that African Americans shopped at. Many Koreans viewed African Americans with suspicion and stereotyped them as potential thieves. Black resentment towards Koreans stemmed from the fact that they provided for the store owners' livelihoods by shopping at their establishments, yet they were overcharged, disrespected, and denied job opportunities, as most Koreans refused to hire them. The Koreans' concerns were not entirely unfounded, as many stores had been robbed on a frequent basis and several of them were in troubled neighborhoods with high crime rates. On the morning of March 16, Soon Ja Du opened Empire Liquor at 9:00 a.m., at a time and place she would not normally be working. A few weeks earlier, her son, Joseph Du, had been robbed by several gang members so naturally, he did not want to work at the store for fear of his life. Empire Liquor, like many stores in South Central L.A., had been robbed multiple times in recent years. Du had good reason to be apprehensive and on edge when she worked in the store and later admitted to having negative feelings towards African Americans in general. When Du saw Harlins place the container of orange juice in her backpack, she automatically assumed it could be for no other reason than theft. As Harlins approached the counter, Du immediately accused her of trying to steal the orange juice and began to pull on her backpack. Harling insisted she was trying to pay for it while Du continued to try and grab her. Harlins then punched Du twice, knocking her down, and then started to walk away. Getting back on her feet, Du then brandished a 38. Caliber Smith and Wesson revolver and fired at Harlins, striking her in the back of the head, killing her instantly. The entire incident had been caught on camera, and two other customers were eyewitnesses to the shooting. Du began to cry out hysterically for her husband, Billy Du, who was resting outside the back of the store in their van, having closed the night before. Authorities then promptly arrived and took Du to the hospital before placing her under arrest for the shooting. Harlins, obviously, was dead on arrival at the hospital. The murder of Harlins, occurring just two weeks after the Rodney King beating, was another shock to Black America in L.A. Still, it was assumed, especially within the Black community, that since both incidents not only had multiple witnesses and were also caught on camera, it would be an open and shut case in court with Du and the officers who assaulted King going to prison. After all, the two instances showed a teenager being shot in the back of the head while walking away from a situation, and a defenseless man being mercilessly beaten, who could not possibly pose any threat to those arresting him. How could the outcome be otherwise? If convictions and guilty verdicts could not be easily obtained with these two shocking instances, then surely there was something seriously wrong with the criminal justice system.

Having been indicted by a Grand Jury for the murder of Latasha Harlins, Soon Ja Du had already been released on bail, much to the chagrin of the Harlins family. The trial had been scheduled to be held in Compton in August, but, like the Rodney King trial, a change of venue was granted due to fears that Du would not get a fair trial and fear for her safety. The trial would now be held in downtown L.A. and would not begin until the end of September. Although during the six-month period between the indictment and the trial tensions would remain high, both sides waited to see how the legal process would play out. First, there was the matter of public perception. To many, it seemed that Du had no remorse for the killing of Harlins and that her only real regret was in how it had affected her and her family. To address this issue, it was recommended that the family hire a prominent Black attorney. Charles Lloyd, who had almost thirty years of experience in the courtroom and many favorable rulings to his name, came highly recommended as he had represented numerous Korean clients.

In most high-profile legal cases, the selection of the judge often receives a great deal of attention and scrutiny. In the case of the Harlins trial, the presiding judge had just become a judge, literally. Joyce Ann Karlin had been a successful attorney in both private practice and as an Assistant United States Attorney in Los Angeles before she was appointed a Superior Court judge in early 1991, having served on the bench for just a matter of months at the start of the Harlins trial. From the start, the prosecution believed that the facts clearly showed that Du had deliberately and purposely shot Harlins in the back of the head while she was walking away from the argument. Because of this fact, it was widely assumed that Du could not possibly plead self-defense in the shooting. Du herself did not make a convincing witness as she appeared confused and had to use an interpreter, implying she could not speak English. This was in direct contradiction to eyewitnesses at the store saying she perfectly understood and spoke English fluently. She claimed that she did not know how to fire a gun and did not remember pulling the trigger, even though the store's surveillance video showed her doing just that. To make matters worse for Du, in her interviews with court and probation officials, she came across as unremorseful for her actions and was upset only in relation to how she and her family had been affected, not how Harlin's death had impacted her family and community. She also expressed negative opinions of African Americans and clearly held them in low regard. The defense argued that Du had legitimate reasons to be on edge as Empire Liquor had been robbed multiple times, and her son, Billy Du, himself had been the victim of a robbery very recently. They tried to argue that Harlin's size and the force of her punches alone were enough to make Du feel that her life was in danger.

The prosecution, led by Roxane Carvajal, who was deputy district attorney for Los Angeles County, felt that Judge Karlin clearly sympathized more with Du than the Harlins family and the victim Latasha. This notion was confirmed when, in a stunning turn of events, Karlin forbade the jury to consider a first-degree murder charge, which would have carried the maximum penalty under California law of twenty-five years to life in prison. This development, although an action at the discretion of the presiding judge, struck Carvajal as an abuse of judicial prerogative. In her cross-examination of Du, Carvajal had pointed out that even after Harlins had been shot, Du made no attempt to provide any aid or check on her condition, showing a complete lack of any concern about her. As previously stated, Du had claimed ignorance on how to fire a gun and that she did not intend to shoot, let alone kill Harlins. To those who saw the tape, Carvajal pointed out that these statements simply did not square with what was caught on the surveillance video. Du clearly knew what she was doing, intended to fire the gun, held it in the correct manner, and braced herself against the counter to do so. Du had written Karlin a letter stating that she feared for her life if she was sent to prison because of her high profile because of the murder. Karlin seemed to agree with the defense's assertion that Du genuinely feared for her life when she shot Harlins in the back of the head as she was walking away from her.

After three days of deliberation, the jury delivered a verdict of voluntary manslaughter on October 11, 1991. It was a bitter disappointment to the Harlins family and the Black community. A month later at the sentencing hearing, Judge Karlin, whose sympathy towards Du at this point was well known, pronounced a sentence of five years' probation, 400 hours of community service, a $500 fee, and an order to pay the full expenses of Latasha's funeral. (Cannon. 169. 1997)

In her reasoning for the sentence, Karlin stated that she did not believe Du would pose a further threat to the community and that her family's fear of being robbed had somehow legitimized her attitude towards Harlins. The verdict predictably stunned everyone, especially the Harlins family, who felt it was a major miscarriage of justice. To add insult to injury, in the same letter to Karlin in which she voiced her fears about being imprisoned, Du voiced regret over the killing of Natasia, not Latasha, Harlins, and expressed sympathy for what her long-deceased mother was feeling for her loss. This letter, read aloud by Carvajal during the sentencing hearing, should have laid bare the fact that Soon Ja Du did not care about what she had done and how it had affected the victim's family, or even bothered to learn the details of her victim's correct name and family. It was appalling and offensive beyond words, and even more so that Judge Karlins completely disregarded, or dismissed, it altogether in weighing Du's punishment. Though outraged by the verdict, calm largely prevailed within the Black community. Still, things were on very thin ice between African Americans, Koreans, and the criminal justice system in general. It would not be long before it broke completely, with terrible consequences for all.

From almost the instant the Holliday tape was made public and began airing, it made shockwaves around the world and was played repeatedly during the next thirteen months and beyond. In downtown L.A. at City Hall, Mayor Tom Bradley immediately denounced the officers involved and their actions in the recording. Police Chief Gates also condemned the four officers involved and vowed an investigation. Some felt that Gates had been too quick to condemn his men without having all the facts, causing some resentment. Still, public outrage was so great that it was inevitable that swift indictments would be handed down, followed shortly by a trial where it was assumed that all four men would be swiftly convicted. Or so it was believed.

Eleven days after the beating and four days of Grand Jury deliberations, the District Attorney for Los Angeles County, Ira Reiner, announced the indictments of Stacey Koon, Laurence Powell, Theodore Briseno, and Timothy Wind on March 14, 1991. Now the men would assemble their legal teams, decide their strategy, while a jury was selected and a date set for the trial. However, it would be almost a year before the trial even began due to numerous factors. The first issue that the defense wanted addressed was a change of venue for the trial. It was argued by the defense (each officer had his own attorney representing him) that due to the nature of the trial, it would be difficult for the men to receive a fair trial in the current environment of L.A. Although changing trial venues was a rare occurrence in California history, the request was finally granted by Joan Klein, a California Court of Appeals Justice for the Second District, on July 23, 1991, after it had twice been refused. The other problem faced by the defense was the belief that the presiding Judge first assigned to the case, Bernard Kamins, was biased against the defendants and argued that a change of venue would delay the trial. After it was revealed that Kamins had inappropriately communicated with the prosecution ex parte (one-way communication), the defense filed to have him removed from the trial. Justice Klein agreed, and on August 22, Kamins was formally removed from the case. His replacement would be Judge Stanley Weisberg, who was appointed on November 22, exactly three months after Kamins was dismissed. Four days later, he moved the trial to the East Ventura County Court house in Simi Valley, an hour and a half and roughly fifty miles from downtown L.A. This decision would prove to be as controversial as the trial itself, as Simi Valley is an almost all White community with many of its residents being former police officers. Nevertheless, the trial was finally set to begin in early February 1992 with the selection of the jury.

As jury selection began, it became obvious that there would be few, if any, Black jurors. This was partly because of the demographics of Simi Valley, Ventura County, and partly because most of the potential Black jurors stated on their questionnaires that they had already formed strong opinions on the case and police officers in general. The final jury that was seated was composed of residents who, by and large, had positive opinions about the police and their role in the community. The composition of the jury was certainly encouraging for the defense as it consisted of six men and six women (one male had been excused and replaced by an alternate shortly after the trial began) of whom ten were white, one Latino, one Asian, and no Black jurors at all. The prosecution was led by Deputy District Attorney Terry White, and as previously stated, each officer had his own attorney. With the jury seated, the trial known as *People vs. Powell* got underway on March 5, 1992. Although all four officers were on trial facing serious charges, it was believed that Powell was the defendant most likely to face conviction since he had landed most of the baton strikes on King and was the most active officer in the Holliday tape. From the opening arguments, the defense for Laurence Powell, led by Michael Stone, a former LAPD officer turned attorney, argued that Powell had acted according to use-of-force guidelines and had done his duty in subduing a violent suspect, possibly under the influence of PCP as well as alcohol. This belief that the arrest had been conducted properly based on established procedure was taken as gospel by Sgt. Koon, who had directed the arrest. Koon's attorney, Darryl Mounger, made his opening arguments by portraying his client as a dedicated, thoughtful, and professional police officer who escalated the force against King also according to procedure and at no point had lost control or acted with malice towards King. Just as importantly, he, along with Stone, made the founding argument that the only person responsible for what had happened to King was Rodney King himself. After all, was it not King who had decided to drink and drive, engage in a high-speed chase with police, and then refuse to follow verbal commands and resist arrest? It only helped to foster the perception of King as irresponsible and out of control when the prosecution had decided not to call him a witness. King had never been able to really account for his actions during and after the arrest. His personality itself was somewhat bizarre and erratic to say the least, and he could never keep his story of the events of March 3, 1991, coherent. Still, for the Jury, despite its pro-police orientation, to see and hear King in his own words and to, hopefully, view him as a person being mercilessly beaten might have aroused some sympathy from the jurors.

As the first of the defendants to take the stand, Stacey Koon, as the man in charge of the arrest, would also prove to be the best. All throughout his testimony, Sgt. Koon was even keeled, recalled facts from all aspects of the arrest, and justified all his decisions involving the use of force. Of note was Koon's insistence that all officers on the scene holster their sidearms to de-escalate the situation, stating that this action was per his training from the Police Academy. He also admitted that the arrest was violent and expressed regret for what had to be done, in his opinion, to make King compliant so he could be taken into custody. As would become commonplace throughout the trial, Koon would stand in front of a TV set used to replay the Holiday video and dissect, second by second and frame by frame, the entire eighty-two second clip. Mounger believed that by going into so much detail over the video, it would impress upon the jury that Koon did not have the luxury of analyzing every possible course of action during the arrest and that he had to react as best he could.

Upon being cross-examined by Deputy District Attorney Alan Yochelson, Koon again stuck to the same story about the details of the arrest and conceded once again that the arrest had been exceedingly violent yet necessary. Koon's most powerful moment came when asked by Mounger what was going through his head the moment he saw California Highway Patrol Officer Melanie Singer approaching King with her gun drawn. Koon responded by relating a story of when he was in training at the academy, "They show a picture when you are in the academy [taken] at the morgue, and it is four [highway patrol] officers in full uniform that are on a slab and they are dead, and it is the Newhall shooting." (Cannon. p. 213. 1997) The Newhall shooting was a violent confrontation in April 1970 when five California Highway Patrol officers died in a gruesome shootout with two heavily armed assailants. As he neared the end of this statement, Koon's voice broke as he fought back tears, recalling the incident. If the prosecution had hoped to portray Sgt. Stacey Koon as a callous or incompetent Police Sergeant who had lost control of the situation, then they had failed. If anything, Koon came across as genuine, professional, and a man of honesty. Koon's testimony itself had dramatically increased TV viewership of the trial from 190,000 households to an additional 390,000. (Koon p. 180. 1992)

The next witness to be called was a boon to the defense's case, that the officers had used force in a controlled and proper manner. Sgt. Charles Duke, a long-time LAPD SWAT officer, was a use-of-force trainer whose credentials were well known and respected. Duke walked through the procedures and steps that the officers had used during the attempt to subdue King. He pointed out that, according to the videotape, the officers were not just wailing away with their batons but also stepping back and evaluating their effectiveness against King while giving him the chance to comply with orders to surrender. Duke's testimony also helped make the case that, had the chokehold not been banned, the officers would have had an alternative to take King into custody without beating him into submission.

    After Sgt. Duke, the next major witness was Laurence Powell. From the start, Stone had mixed feelings about putting Powell on the stand. His somewhat abrasive and excitable nature might not play very well with the jury as it would show him to be unsteady, especially in a high-pressure situation like the King arrest. However, Powell's nervousness as he recounted the arrest seemed to play favorably with the jury as they could see that the incident clearly unnerved him. Like Sgt. Koon Powell spoke of King's immense size and how scared he was when he simply tossed him and the other officers off his back during the initial attempt to take him into custody. The impression of Powell's fear of King helped to cement the belief among the jury that Powell, however poorly he used his P24-baton, was not acting out of malice but out of a genuine fear for his life. Under cross-examination by the prosecution, White attempted to paint Powell's response and attitude towards King as racist. To support this argument, White pointed to Powell's computer messages to other officers after the incident stating he, "hadn't beaten anyone this bad in a long time" as well as the previously mentioned message referring to a domestic disturbance between an African American couple by stating, "It was a scene right out of Gorillas in the Mist." White, who is African American, repeatedly tried to get Powell to admit that his comments were of a racial nature and showed his true attitude towards African Americans. Another matter of contention was Powell's steadfast denial that his first baton strike had hit King in the face despite eyewitness accounts to the contrary. As the cross-examination continued, White's irritation with Powell became more apparent as he implied that Powell's actions and attitude suggested that he was simply a poorly trained and sadistic Police Officer. Although

Powell would deny having racist attitudes and continued to contest that his first baton strike landed on King's Chest, White did manage to score points by making him appear to be a). unwilling to accept any responsibility for what he had done, b). that his baton strikes might have been excessive and c). his attitude towards the King was callous and cruel. It could not have been lost on the courtroom that White's contempt for Powell, and it would certainly not be the last time he would lose his temper with him.

Theodore Briseno's contention that the amount of force used in the arrest was excessive and unjustified had placed him at odds with his fellow officers and had got him branded as a traitor. Briseno's attorney, John Barnett, sought to portray him as a veteran officer who saw that the situation had gotten out of control and tried to stop it. During the arrest, and before any baton strikes, Briseno had been among the group of officers attempting to swarm King and handcuff him and was subsequently thrown off by King. After Sgt. Koon's taser shots had no effect on King, Briseno was close at hand as first Powell and then Wind began striking King with their batons.

Once on the stand, Briseno performed solidly and stood in front of the TV screen where the video was played throughout the trial, describing in detail, frame by frame and second by second, how he thought the arrest had gone wrong. Answering every question put to him with "yes, sir", he exuded an air of politeness yet firmness. After King had rushed Powell and had been knocked down by his initial baton strike, Powell and then Wind began to strike King repeatedly. After the first flurry of baton strikes from Powell and Wind had momentarily ceased, Briseno had stepped towards Powell and pushed him back with his left arm to stop him from striking King anymore. According to Briseno, at this point, he could not see why it was necessary to continue beating King in this manner, as he could not possibly pose a threat. Over and over, he would describe Powell as "out of control". When asked by Barnett what he was thinking at this moment during the arrest, Briseno articulated that he was trying to understand what Powell and Wind might be thinking and how it could justify any additional force. He speculated that maybe they might have seen something he did not, such as King having a weapon that had eluded his notice. After yet another round of baton strikes, Briseno, now repositioned, claimed he had stated out loud that King's hands were free, hoping this would reassure the other officers that he was unarmed. As King lay down, still unresponsive to verbal commands, Briseno then put his left foot on King's left shoulder to keep him down so he could be handcuffed. King, however continued to move, and Powell and Wind resumed striking him. At this point, Briseno then states he walks up to Sgt. Koon and asks, "What the Fuck is going on here?" only to be met with no response. The ordeal finally ended with King placing his hands on his head, and Briseno, along with several other officers, handcuffing him. Briseno then claimed that once he was back inside his squad car he unloaded on his partner, probationary officer Rolando Solano who became a bystander after the first attempt to swarm King had failed, stating, "Goddamn, sergeant should have handled this a lot differently. He should have handled it a lot better…The officers should have their asses reamed." (Cannon. p.232. 1997)

Under cross-examination by the prosecution, White asked Briseno if he thought the use of force was excessive and if he had observed any aggressive or hostile actions by King that would have served as a justification for further use of force. Again, Briseno reiterated that he did not see any behavior on King's part that could be construed as threatening, and his belief that the use of force was excessive. White also questioned whether Briseno had intended to report the incident to the watch commander on duty that night, which he ended up not doing when he saw a computer message from Sgt. Koon is on the Lieutenant's office computer. The testimony of Briseno had cast major doubts over the notion that the use of force was measured and according to procedure. Still, Briseono was questioned by White whether he knew about the "code of silence" among Police Officers and would have been a party to it regarding this incident, which he denied he would. Briseno's performance on the stand had been solid enough, but whether it would convince the jury he had acted out of concern for King and tried to stop the beating was yet to be seen. Nevertheless, Briseno had long been labeled a traitor by his fellow officers for not showing solidarity with them over the incident.

After almost two months, the testimony of fifty-five witnesses and the video itself being replayed over and over and analyzed frame by frame at full and half speed, as well as countless pauses, the time had come for closing arguments. During his three-and-a-half-hour closing argument, White focused almost exclusively on Powell and his actions. He drew attention to the fact that Powell had made several "lies" repeatedly throughout his police report on the incident, citing his claims of several near traffic accidents while in pursuit of King that did not occur, as well as his contention that King was likely on PCP, which was never conclusively proven. Next, he zeroed in on several of Powell's recollections of the arrest, especially his refusal to concede that his first baton strike was intentional and landed on King's face, and then his actions at the hospital where he taunted King while he was treated for his injuries. Again and again, he hammered on the point that Powell's use of force was unjustified and that King posed no threat. White once again brought attention to Powell's computer messages about the arrest and the prior one referring to a feuding Black couple as Gorillas as evidence of Powell's bigotry and callousness. Later during the rebuttal, when describing how none of Powell's behavior or actions was ever his fault (according to his testimony and Michael Stone) or how he never took responsibility, White momentarily lost his composure, briskly walked to over to Powell pointed at him and shouted, "This is the man-and look at him. This man laughed. This man taunted." before being ordered to return to the podium by Judge Weisberg. (Cannon. p.250. 1997) He then closed by playing the eighty-two-second video all the way through at full speed and asked the jury to trust their own eyes as to whether the use of force was justified and whether all four defendants were guilty.

Although all the defense lawyers made the same argument asking the jurors to see the situation through the eyes of the officers, had they been in their shoes, they also made arguments specific to their own client. Michael Stone argued that Laurence Powell had acted according to procedure and had followed the orders of Sgt. Stacey Koon and had done his duty. While he had made errors in his police report of the incident, he was hardly the only officer who ever did so, and it (the police report) had been made in good faith. In his closing argument on behalf of Timothy Wind, who was the only officer not to testify, Paul DePasquale stated that Wind, too, had simply done his job and that Rodney King had been a "problem" that Wind had to deal with. Speaking on behalf of Theodore Briseno, John Barnett attacked the "code of silence" culture among officers that seeks to keep police misconduct from coming to light and stated that Briseno was a victim of it. He argued that Briseno, rather than being an accomplice to the beating, had in good conscience seen that it was wrong and had tried to stop it, spoken to a watch commander about it, and had paid dearly for breaking ranks with his fellow officers. Darryl Mounger reiterated that Sergeant Stacey Koon was a competent and professional officer who had responded to a situation the best he could with what he had at the time. He reminded the jury that had it not been for Koon, Rodney King might have been shot the night of his arrest, as Koon had ordered all officers present to holster their side arms before they tried to take him into custody. Most importantly, it was King who was to blame for what had happened, not any of the officers involved, as his speeding and subsequent actions were what caused the escalating use of force in his arrest. The morning after White's rebuttal, Judge Weisberg outlined for the jury guidelines to use when deciding their verdict for the case and then promptly sequestered them. Now, Los Angeles, and the world, waited.

Deputy District Attorney Terry White felt alarmed when reading potential jurors' questionnaires when jury selection was still underway two months ago. Now, as the jury began their deliberations, it seemed his worst fears were confirmed. As stated earlier, there were no Black jurors on the jury. Of the twelve jurors that comprised the jury, three were members of the National Rifle Association (NRA), two were retired veterans, and almost all had expressed attitudes favorable towards police officers. Jury foreman, sixty-four-year-old Dorothy Bailey, had epitomized this attitude when recounting her first impressions of the principals in a later interview. Of Terry White, the lead prosecutor, she stated that she was "not particularly impressed" as she felt him to be, "overly dramatic and very emotional in his presentation. It seemed like an act for me, like he was putting on a show for us." (Neumeyer, 2017) Another telling fact was her professed shock that Briseno would testify that he thought his fellow officers were guilty and that his lawyer, John Barnet, "sounded as if he were part of the prosecution. In short order, Briseno, Koon, and Wind were all acquitted of the charges against them in the space of just two days. Most tellingly, the charges against Koon and Powell for filing false reports were also dismissed. The jurors had seemingly bought Koon's and the defense's assertion that Rodney King's bizarre behavior, non-compliance, and massive size had made the beating necessary.

Still, despite the overwhelming bias toward law enforcement and the rapid dismissal of all but one charge, there were three jurors who felt strongly enough that the use of force by Powell was unlawful and excessive. Anna Whiting fifty-four, Virginia Loya forty, also the only Hispanic juror, and Kevin Siminski thirty-eight, all expressed doubts as to whether Powell's baton strikes were lawful and constituted deadly force. They articulated that, unlike Wind, who could be seen stepping back to evaluate the effects of his baton strikes, Powell had made no such effort and kept wailing away. Despite arguments back and forth, only one juror changed his mind. Christopher Morgan, forty-three, decided to vote with the dissenting three to convict Powell of assault under color of authority. The jury was now deadlocked 8-4 on the final remaining charge, having dismissed the other ten.

After seven days of deliberations, on Wednesday April 29, 1992, Judge Weisberg was informed that the jury had reached verdicts on all but one of the eleven charges against the defendants. Having delayed an announcement of the verdict for two hours to give LAPD time to prepare for any potential disturbances, Weisberg was presented the verdicts by foreman Bailey at 3:00 p.m. PST. All parties in the courtroom, in Los Angeles, the country, and the world collectively held their breath to hear the conclusion of one of the most controversial and emotional trials in American history. The media, Police Chief Gates, Mayor Bradley, the Black community, and even the defendants and their attorneys had expected guilty verdicts. It had been taken for granted among so many people that the Holliday tape was so damning that nothing other than a guilty verdict could be the only possible outcome. Having read the verdict,

Weisberg then handed it to the clerk, who proceeded to announce that the defendants had been found not guilty ten times. A sense of disbelief and profound shock began to rapidly reverberate throughout the courtroom, the crowd outside, Simi Valley, California, the whole nation, the whole world and especially in South Central L.A. Dorothy Bailey had summed up the jury's reasoning by stating, "In my opinion it's not right or morally acceptable to beat any human being, but if LAPD policy has determined its right in certain circumstances, we had to go with that and we did." (Cannon. p. 255. 1997) Legalities aside, Black America saw that it was ok to beat a man senseless and that those responsible would suffer no consequences. The drama in the courtroom was finally over; now it moved into the streets. With a vengeance.

Film director John Singleton, who was in the court audience at Simi Valley when the verdict was read, said correctly that, "By having this verdict, what these people have done, they lit the fuse to a bomb." Singleton's words could not have been more prescient, for after the riots were over, a bomb might as well have exploded. Across L.A., almost everyone was stunned and shocked by the verdicts, but none more so than the inhabitants of South-Central L.A. Crowds had started to form all over the city as an air of unease and anxiety prevailed all around. By now, it was obvious that something sinister and menacing was in the air, and all the pent-up rage that African Americans had felt from the trial and the Harlins case was about to explode. News media were present in great numbers, and people interviewed were only too happy to share their opinions. One Black man interviewed outside the courtroom shouted emotionally, "I'm glad that you guys showed this to the world to let them see how Black people are treated in this country. We've been here [America] for 437 years and we don't get nothing." (National Geographic, 2017)

After receiving the verdicts, a sullen Mayor Bradley made a brief statement at City Hall where he said, "Today this jury told the world that what we all saw with our own eyes wasn't a crime. Today, the jury asked us to accept the senseless and brutal beating of a helpless man. Today, the jury said that we tolerate such conduct by those who are sworn to protect and serve. My friends, I'm here to tell this jury no. No, our eyes did not deceive us. We saw what we saw. And what we saw was a crime." A large crowd had congregated at the AME Church, the oldest African American Church in the city. Speaker after speaker, from Mayor Bradley, city council members, and the church's own Rev. Cecil Murray, pleaded with congregants to "even in anger, be cool". The crowd gathering outside did not share this sentiment. Not this time. One man summed up the mood by stating, "They in there talkin about peace. Every time we talk about peace, we get a foot in our ass." (National Geographic, 2017) There were too many times that they had been told to be patient, to let the system dispense justice, and to have faith in that process. The time for the courtroom had passed. Now, the only means of recourse was the streets. Brenda Wall, PhD., would describe the psychology of the rioters when she wrote, "The psychology of racism damages the targeted victim. Many of those who rioted felt powerless and expressed their overwhelming frustration and helplessness in an uncontrollable rage and an effort to demonstrate personal and collective power." (Wall. p.18.1992) The next five days would show how accurate this description was.

One hour after the verdicts were announced, about 4:00 p.m., the police were called to respond to a robbery reported at the Payless Liquor and Deli store, which was located at the intersection of Florence and Dalton Ave. Five Black youths had just stolen several beers from the store and assaulted the owner's son as he tried to stop them. By the time the first officers reached the scene, the assailants were long gone, and there was already another disturbance nearby involving a youth swinging a baseball bat at a parked car, who was quickly apprehended. The officers who remained behind then pursued another Black youth who approached them with rocks in his hands. Other officers patrolling close by were also subjected to attacks by rocks, bottles, and anything that could make an effective projectile as the gathering crowds turned ever more hostile. After the arrest of two more Black men for throwing rocks at and attempting to assault officers (which by now numbered over thirty after a call for assistance had been made by officers already on the scene) Lieutenant Michael Moulin of the 77th division LAPD, ordered all personnel in the Florence and Normandie area to pull back around 5:45 p.m. The intersection of Florence and Normandie, where the assaults on passing motorists and police first began, would see wanton destruction and brutality become the norm over the next five days as property and mostly non-Black people were attacked with utter impunity and savagery. The police, outnumbered and powerless to stop the mob growing and ferocity by the minute, had effectively ceded the area to them.

As the city began to go up in flames and tear itself apart, Chief Gates inexplicably left Police headquarters at the Parker Center downtown to attend a political function in nearby Brentwood to campaign against what was known as Charter Amendment F. The amendment was a recommendation by the Christopher Commission in the wake of the King beating that sought to limit a Police Chief's time in office. For a man who had shown time and again that he was a dedicated police officer who was willing to go against public opinion to do what he thought was right, this decision, almost more than any other, showed how out of touch Gates had become with the situation on the ground. His refusal prior to the verdict to order a tactical alert in case of major disturbances and have police out in force on the streets along with the elite METRO units demonstrated a staggering lack of judgment. Like most people, he was certain there would be guilty verdicts and thought a heavy police presence would have been overly provocative.

As the LAPD and Gates continued to debate their response to the riots, many officers felt a sense of helplessness at the situation. After the pullout from Florence and Normandie, all elements of the 77th Division began to gather at a bus depot nearby at 54th and Arlington Ave. in preparation for what many believed would be an effort to retake the intersection. Meanwhile, events continued to deteriorate at a rapid rate throughout all South-Central L.A. At Florence and Normandie, all traffic passing through the intersection was subjected to verbal abuse and having all manner of projectiles thrown at them. If the motorists happened to be Black, they were allowed to pass unharmed. If they were White, Latino, or Asian, then they were in grave danger. Countless motorists were forced out of their vehicles and viciously assaulted while cameras from participants on the ground and police/news helicopters filmed their ordeal, while powerless to help. At 6:45 P.M., just over an hour after Lt. Moulin had ordered a withdrawal from the Florence and Normandie area, thirty-nine-year-old truck driver Reginald Denny, unaware of the riots, was approaching the intersection when he noticed the disturbances up ahead. Before he could respond or try to think about turning around, he was pulled from his cab onto the intersection and beaten by four young Black men. The most notable being one Damian Williams, also known as "football" to his friends. During the assault, Denny received several blows, kicks, and also had a cinder block broken over his head by Williams, which left him unconscious and barely alive. Like King's arrest, Denny's beating horrified the nation. Sheer anarchy now reigned supreme in Florence and Normandie. As nightfall approached, the chaos only seemed to be spreading with no sign of LAPD or anyone able to stop it.

In the capital city of Sacramento, Governor Pete Wilson held a brief press conference where he affirmed the state of emergency declared by Mayor Bradley and mobilized the California National Guard to restore order. As the rioting continued into the next day, Thursday, April 30, a new threat emerged to the residents and business owners: mass looting. With the National Guard yet to deploy and local law enforcement still largely absent, residents took carte blanche to take whatever was available, or what they wanted, from deserted stores. The group that was most likely to be targeted more than others was the South Korean store owners scattered all throughout South Central.

Recognizing that help was unlikely to come from LAPD, the South Koreans armed themselves, banded together, and defended their property bravely in horrific gunfights against the rioters and looters using everything from AK-47s to Uzis and regular handguns. Unlike the rest of the city, they would not let their livelihoods and property simply be destroyed and looted. At least not without a fight. Richard Rhee, owner of the California Market in Koreatown, stated as much when he said, "Burn this down after thirty-three years? They don't know how hard I've worked. This is my market and I'm going to protect it." (Cannon. p. 335. 1997) Over the next three days, similar scenes played out across Koreatown as the store owners were aided by Radio Korea (KBLA), which broadcast movements of looters and helped coordinate defense among the community. (Sumi K. Cho/ Williams. p. 201. 1993) Unfortunately, many business owners and residents were not as fortunate as the Koreans and lacked the arms to defend themselves. When approached by mobs of rioters, their only course of action was to stand by and watch as their livelihoods were destroyed.

Throughout April 30, there was an increased presence of police in the city, and although looting ceased in their immediate area of deployment, they were simply too few and the looters and rioters too many to have any significant impact. As soon as the police moved on, the rioters returned, and the looting resumed. Much to Chief Gate's mounting frustration, it had become evident that LAPD was incapable of responding in force to the riots, much less containing them. A dusk-to-dawn curfew that had been put into effect by Mayor Bradley at midnight on April 30 had little effect in deterring the rioters and looters. With many structures set ablaze due to arson, destruction had become widespread. Firefighters could only respond to fires when they had police escorts to ensure their safety, which were few and far between. There were many instances of engine and ladder crews being harassed, assaulted, and even shot at by rioters. Although LAPD had managed to erect barriers sealing off South Central from other neighborhoods in the city, the staging area at 54th and Arlington Ave. was just that. A simple staging area. No effort would be made to retake Florence and Normandie. Rioters and looters had more to fear from Korean store owners and those individuals who took matters into their own hands than the LAPD.

By the third day of rioting on May 1, the man in whose name all this destruction had taken place decided he could remain silent no longer. Appearing with his attorney, Steve Lerman, in front a camera, Rodney Glen King, the man whom most Americans only knew of as a grainy image on a home video that showed him being brutally beaten and who had not testified at his own trial, felt compelled to speak out against all the anger and hate that his ordeal had inspired. As Lerman introduced King, he implored, "The killing, the burning, the looting, the chaos, must stop now. The time for healing is upon us. Rodney King has prepared a very brief statement." Appearing shaken and fighting back tears, King simply and elegantly stated, "People, I just want to say, can we get along? Can we all get along? Can we stop making it horrible for the older people and the kids, and I mean, we've got enough smog here in Los Angeles, let alone dealing with setting these fires. It's just not right. It's not right. It's not gonna change anything." King then pleaded, "We can all get along. We're all stuck here for a while. Let's try to work it out. Let's just try to work it out." (National Geographic, 2017)

Later that evening, President Bush addressed the nation, informing them of his decision to federalize the California National Guard and send Marines and Soldiers to the city to assist in providing security and restoring order. As this was the most pressing issue, he announced the deployment of over a thousand law enforcement officials with special training in riot control from various agencies. He then stated that 3,000 soldiers of the 7th Infantry Division and 1,500 Marines were on standby should they be needed to assist the 3,000 National Guardsmen already on patrol in the city. The President then stated that the riot was "The brutality of a mob. Pure and simple. And let me assure you, I will use whatever force is necessary to restore order. What is going on in L.A. must and will stop." He then announced that a federal investigation had begun into the beating of Rodney King and federal prosecutors had already been dispatched to California and assured Americans that justice would be done. Returning to the theme of law and order, he chastised the rioters once again by saying, "The wanton destruction of life and property is not a legitimate expression of outrage with injustice. It is itself an injustice. And no rationalization, no matter how heartfelt, no matter how eloquent, can make it otherwise. The President then closed by recounting the story of how four Black strangers had helped Reginald Denny drive to the hospital after he was savagely beaten as a showcase of human decency.

With National Guard troops now out in force on the streets and LAPD supplemented by additional law enforcement personnel from several agencies, state and federal, the chaos gradually subsided. On May

4, Mayor Bradley lifted his curfew order, marking the end of the riots. The destruction had been immense and widespread, with over 900 structures destroyed, 2,328 people injured, and 54 fatalities, as well as $900- $1billion in estimated damages. (Cannon. p. 347.1997) In the political realm, both President Bush and Governor Bill Clinton retreated to familiar liberal and conservative themes. The President stressed the need for greater family values and responsibility, along with federal aid in rebuilding the city, as well as a $19 million grant to fight street gangs and drug trafficking. The Governor favored the expansion of enterprise zones, colloquially known as "weed and seed" projects. (Gale.p.109-110.1996) Both men would make visits to South Central after the riots had largely subsided in order to see for themselves the scale of the destruction, although due to security concerns, President Bush's would not be publicized. Still, both the President and the Presidential candidate made appeals for understanding and reconciliation along with repudiation of the violence. To their credit, both men largely kept politics out of public discussion and focused on recovery.

Riot victims saw firsthand how righteous anger over the verdicts ended up destroying their homes, businesses, and communities. In the wake of the riots, mass arrests were conducted with many citizens helping police identify those who took part. Chief Gates himself would personally arrest Damian Williams for the beating of Reginald Denny, his last career arrest. Despite all the post-riot rhetoric about understanding and tolerance, people's attitudes about each other and the trial only seemed to get worse.

Like many institutions of higher learning, the University of California, Los Angeles, annually conducts social surveys on a variety of topics and issues to gauge public opinion and attitudes for residents of Los Angeles County. A sample group of African Americans, Whites, Asians, and Hispanics was asked how they felt about the verdicts. Out of 437 African Americans, 75.7 % strongly disagreed (with 20.6% simply disagreeing) while only .5% strongly agreed with 1.4% agreeing. Out of 372 Whites polled, 32.3% strongly disagreed with the acquittals (with 32.8% simply disagreeing) while 17.25% agreed, with 4.0% strongly agreeing. With the statement that African Americans do not receive fair treatment from the criminal justice system 44.2% of African Americans out of 425 polled strongly agreed with 35.5% simply agreeing, while only 11.1% disagreed with 3.1% strongly disagreeing. Out of 202 Asians polled, only 8.4% strongly agreed, 7.9% of Hispanics out of 466, and 9.2% of Whites out of 370 polled on the question of African Americans not receiving fair treatment in the criminal justice system. On the question of whether the riots were viewed as either a form of protest or simply looting and street crime, 67.5% of African Americans felt they were mainly protesting, while only 22.8% saw them as simple crime along with looting out of 412 polled. Out of 196 Asians polled 42.9% saw the riots as a form of mainly protest, while 50.5% saw them as looting and street crime. Among 470 Hispanics, 38.7% percent saw them as a protest while 51.9% saw them as looting and street crime. Finally, out of 364 Whites polled, 37.4% saw them as a form of protest, while 55.8% saw them as looting and street crime. Most tellingly on this last question, between Asians, African Americans, Hispanics, and Whites, only 6.6%, 9.7%, 9.4% and 6.9% respectively, saw the riots as a mixture of protest and looting. (Baldassare. p. 111. 1994) A poll on ethnic relations that had been fielded twelve weeks prior to and after the verdicts found that only 9.5% of Asians felt African Americans were easy to get along with, down from a 20.8% pre-trial. Even more upsetting was that 64.9% of Asians thought African Americans to be less intelligent as opposed to 59.2% pre-trial. (Baldassare. p. 117. 1994) The aftermath of the riots had made it painfully clear that any sort of meaningful reconciliation and healing would take time to become a reality.

The fallout from the riots even impacted the upcoming Presidential election. Rap artist and activist Sista Soulja had recently drawn controversy for the lyrics in her song "The Final Solution: Slavery's Back in Effect," in which she stated, "Remember the times when they bought and they sold ya? WE ARE AT War!! That's what I told ya!!" The music video for the song graphically portrays police officers being shot and bloodied, with African Americans resisting being taken back into slavery. Soulja (born Lisa Williamson) was known for incendiary afro-centric political rhetoric and was no stranger to controversy, having stated in one interview that he had never met any good white people. In a subsequent interview with the Washington Post on May 13, 1992, Soulja had made the remarks, "If black people kill black people every day, then why not have a week and kill white people."

At a speaking engagement on June 13, 1992, at the Rainbow Coalition, an organization run by the Rev. Jesse Jackson, presumptive democratic nominee Arkansas Gov. Bill Clinton made what some saw as either a courageous repudiation of an extremist artist or a politically calculating move to appeal to suburban white moderates he would need come November. Regardless of his intentions, Clinton's statement resonated in the exact manner he wanted and needed it to. Taking the podium with Jesse Jackson sitting to his left, Clinton lambasted Soulja by stating, "If you took the words 'white' and 'black' and reversed them, you might think David Duke (a Louisiana politician and former Grand Wizard of the Ku Klux Klan) was giving that speech." Clinton then went on to admit, as Soulja would charge, that he had played golf at an all-white country club in Arkansas but had resolved never to do so again. He then went on to implore that the democrats would not be able to win if they keep being divided over race and to urge unity. Clinton had what came to be known as his "Sista Soulja moment," as would other politicians in the future, notably Barack Obama, in denouncing his former pastor Reverend Jeremiah Wright after some of his inflammatory sermons and comments came to light during the 2008 presidential campaign.

Throughout the 1980s, Jackson had been perceived as the embodiment of the far-left, radical race-based politics. In 1984 and 1988, he had waged two credible campaigns for the democratic presidential nomination, and although he was considered toxic to moderate voters and was given little chance at winning, he had won several primary contests, registered large numbers of new voters, and had prominent speaking slots at several national conventions. In 1988, he had briefly been considered the front-runner for the nomination and had given the eventual nominee, Massachusetts Gov. Michael Dukakis, a run for his money. Jackson's influence within the Democratic Party and with African Americans was immense. Many figures in democratic politics had refused to stand up to Jackson or to call him out on his occasionally over the top rhetoric, particularly in 1988, treating him as Georgia Gov. Zell Miller would lament, "with kid gloves no matter what he said. No matter how outrageous or extreme. No one would ever question or confront him." (Miller. p. 217. 2003) Clinton's rebuke had sent a message that he would not be intimidated by Jackson nor hesitate to stand up to fringe figures within the Democratic Party fold, much to the delight of Gov. Miller and others, while to the chagrin of Jackson and Soulja. It was also in keeping with his moderate new democrat image that he was hoping would carry him to the White House.

In light of the riots and all the ensuing destruction, it was hard to argue that artists such as Soulja, Ice-T, Tupac, and others did not accurately reflect the anger and hopelessness that many African Americans had long felt in South Central L.A. and inner cities across the country. As history has shown time and again, when people are marginalized and feel that the institutions of their society not only do not serve them but actively seek to harm them, then what alternative would they, or anyone, express themselves other than by violence and destruction? The feelings of older Black Americans who had lived through the chaos and violence of the Civil Rights movement in the 1960s were one of continuing cynicism and doubt as to whether any positive change would result from the riots. Veteran Civil Rights leader and Reverend. Wyatt Tee Walker of Canaan Baptist Church in Harlem, N.Y., did not believe there would be any substantial change in either government policy or white attitudes towards black people . He stated, "Not much is going to come from another guilt trip for White America. It is going to come only from a commitment to justice. But white America has never made that commitment. Until it does, these little flashes of conscience rending are not going to change anything." (Grieder, 1992) The same cycle of commission upon commission, leading to promises made and promises not kept, is not easily, if ever, forgotten.

Although acquitted in the state trial, at the behest of President Bush, an investigation was launched at the federal level with charges once again filed against the four officers. This time, Rodney King testified, and two guilty verdicts were returned against Koon and Powell while Briseno and Wind were again acquitted in March 1993. Stacey Koon, Laurence Powell, Theodore Briseno, and Timothy Wind would never work as police officers again. In the coming years, they would all have to contend with difficulty finding employment, having their reputations permanently ruined, and death threats, among other things. On June 27, 1992, Daryl Gates stepped down as Chief of Police of Los Angeles after fourteen years of service and over forty years as a police officer in general. Mayor Tom

Bradley resigned just over a year later on July 1, 1993, twenty years to the day after he first became mayor. Both Bradley and Gates had seen their public image damaged as a result of the riots, and it was hoped among many that their replacements would turn the page and start a new chapter for the city. Fears of racial violence would once again sweep Los Angeles and the country when football star O.J. Simpson was arrested and tried for the murder of his ex-wife, Anna Nicole Simpson throughout 1995. Although Simpson was found not guilty on October 3, 1995, state officials this time would not be caught flat-footed as they were three and a half years ago. Contingency plans at the state and federal levels were drawn up and put in place in case they were needed. Fortunately, this time they were not.

It cannot be overlooked that the role that technology played in the drama of Rodney King, the trial, the riots, and all that followed. One man, George Holliday, and his Sony Video8 Handycam CCD-F77 brought to the public's consciousness what so many thought to be an isolated incident of police brutality. In reality, what happened to Rodney King was not an abnormal experience for Black people dealing with law enforcement. That it was captured on tape and showed the entire arrest in all its graphic detail was. The American public, and the world, saw what showed a Black man on the ground, surrounded by police officers mercilessly striking him with batons, being kicked, and subdued. In an era where such portable devices were becoming widely used, anyone ideally positioned could be in a position to film an event of great significance. During the riots, several rioters, news media, and police would also be filming events that brought the grisly reality of the disturbances home to audiences around the world. The most shocking of all these was the horrific beating of truck driver Reginald Denny at the intersection of Florence and Normandie, as well as others, by circling police and news helicopters.

1992

Almost thirty years later, another instance of police brutality would once again capture the world's attention and lead to mass protest, violence, and widespread destruction. However, unlike the Rodney King incident, this one would prove to be fatal for the man involved in the altercation, one Mr. George Perry Floyd Jr. On May 25, 2020, four Minneapolis police officers were called to a grocery store when it was suspected that Mr. Floyd might be using a counterfeit $20 bill. Once the officers arrived, they handcuffed Floyd and Officer Derek Chauvin, who had been the subject of eighteen complaints during his police career, knelt on George Floyd's neck for over nine minutes while Floyd repeatedly stated that he could not breathe. Floyd was pronounced dead en route to the hospital in the ambulance. Like the Rodney King incident, the murder of Floyd was caught on film, but this time with multiple cell phone cameras as well as surveillance cameras from several buildings nearby. Perhaps the most notable difference between 1991 and 2020 was the by then universal use of body cameras on police officers that provided a first-person view from the officer's perspective. Several bystanders urged Chauvin to remove his knee from Floyd's neck as he grew unresponsive while also filming the incident.

The news of Floyd's death rapidly went viral, causing instant outrage and unrest. Whereas the Rodney King riots had occurred mainly in the Los Angeles area and lasted about a week, the George Floyd ones would be worldwide and ongoing throughout the summer of 2020 and beyond, costing an estimated $2 billion in damages. Had he somehow survived, one does wonder if Floyd would have made a similar appeal like King in 1992 for calm and non-violence. Regardless of the criminal records of both King and Floyd, the power of video shows the complete and naked cruelty that both men endured. One survived. One did not. More commissions, more investigations, more firings, more promises, body cameras on officers, and statistics to show how things had changed. Time and again, the courts had sided with the officers in question, placed them on paid administrative leave, maybe fired or let them resign, etc. All of it meant nothing. Absolutely nothing. For as far as Black America was concerned. It had happened. Again. Latasha Harlins, Rodney King. Amadou Diallo, Eric Garner, Michael Brown, Philando Castile, Freddie Gray, Breonna Taylor, and not last but most notably, George Floyd, along with countless others, caught up in the ensuing violence. Black families still had to have "the talk" with their children about dealing with law enforcement. Being told not to run and cooperate even when they, and everyone else, could see with their own eyes what that would likely get them. Having heard first-hand the experiences of their peers, parents, and seeing on television and the internet the same tragedy over and over again, how could they not ask themselves, Will I ever be safe? Are the police on my side? Have things changed? Will they ever?

1992

Rodney King, whose brutal March 1991 beating by LAPD Officers Koon, Powell, Wind, and Briseno touched off a firestorm of racial unrest not seen since the 1960s.

The April 29, 1992, acquittal of the four officers involved in King's beating resulted in five days of rioting and chaos before order was restored.

CHAPTER 6

The World Over: Earth Summit in Rio, Free Trade, etc.

In many ways, 1992 saw the world becoming increasingly interconnected, especially in the realm of technology, international trade, and the environment. With the Cold War over, the developed and developing nations of the world began to turn their attention towards issues of sustainability and the impact that energy use, mainly fossil fuels, was having on the global environment. This, in turn, led to questions of how to develop, harness, and use renewable forms of energy for greater use in the future. Also of major concern were issues of economic development and conservation of natural resources. From June 3-14, 1992, all of these issues and many others were debated and discussed in an unprecedented meeting of 178 nations in Rio de Janeiro, Brazil, for the first-ever United Nations Conference on Environment and Development (UNCED) or also known as the Earth Summit.

Environmental awareness was nothing new by 1992. The first UN-sponsored environmental summit was held in Stockholm, Sweden, from June 5-16, 1972. Issues that were discussed at the United Nations Conference on the Human Environment revolved mainly around resource conservation and reducing pollution. In an echo of future summits, many developing countries harshly criticized the developed ones for everything from the overuse of resources, imperialism, and exploitation of their former colonies. Nevertheless, the Stockholm conference was the first worldwide effort to address a variety of environmental issues. Two years earlier, the first Earth Day had been proclaimed on April 22, 1970, to increase conservation and environmental awareness in the United States and worldwide. Later that year, US President Richard Nixon established the Environmental Protection Agency (EPA) to reduce industrial pollution and enforce various rules and regulations.

Throughout the 1980's a series of environmental disasters and crises occurred across the world, raising awareness of the need for the international community to act in concert to address them. On April 26, 1986, number four reactor at the Chernobyl nuclear facility in the Soviet Union (present day Ukraine) exploded during a test simulation, resulting in the worst nuclear disaster in history. Occurring only seven years after the Three Mile Island disaster in the United States, it drove home the dangers of nuclear power and the necessity of hazardous waste disposal. On March 24, 1989, an American oil tanker, Exxon Valdez, struck a reef in Prince William Sound, Alaska, leaking over 10 million gallons of crude oil, resulting in a costly cleanup to thousands of miles of shoreline as well as impacting marine plant and animal life. Perhaps most alarming of all, in the mid-1980s, it was revealed that a massive hole had developed in the Ozone layer, which protects the Earth from the sun's radiation, above Antarctica. This was due to the worldwide use of chlorofluorocarbons (CFCs) found in a variety of machines and products. Despite the severity of the threat to the planet, the world responded effectively. In 1987, at a gathering in Montreal, Canada, forty-six nations created what became known as the Montreal Protocol, designed to phase out the production of

CFCs. Amazingly, it remains the only international treaty ratified by all 198 member nations of the UN to this day and has been a rare success story in the realm of international cooperation.

The success of the Montreal Protocol encouraged the leading nations of the world to seek greater cooperation on issues of environmental and resource allocation, and on December 22, 1989, the United Nations General Assembly passed resolution 44/228 calling for a conference on Environment and Development. Hence, what became known as the Earth Summit or the Rio Conference was to take place in Rio de Janeiro, Brazil, from June 3-14, 1992, after almost three years of preparation. Expectations for the conference were very high. U.S. Senator John Kerry (D-MA) spoke for many when addressing a gathering in Rio de Janeiro as part of the US congressional delegation when he stated, "This conference, this Earth Summit, is going to change the political dynamics of the world." (C-SPAN/Rio) U.S. Senator and soon to be Vice Presidential nominee Al Gore (D-TN) gave an impassioned speech before the Parliamentary Earth Summit, also being held in Rio, on June 5 in which he stated, "so many of us have come to believe as human beings that the ecological crisis, is fundamentally a spiritual crisis." (C-SPAN/Rio) Senator Gore, having long been a champion of environmental issues, had recently published a book, Earth in the Balance: Ecology and the Human Spirit, in which he called for a Strategic Environment Initiative (SEI). This entailed tax incentives for companies to develop environmentally friendly technology, along with export controls in developed nations to assess a technology's potential effectiveness before it is shipped overseas, as well as stronger legal protections for inventors. (Gore. p.320.1992)

The conference was to be chaired by Maurice Strong of Canada, a diplomat with a long career at the UN and a man of great environmental expertise. In addition to speeches from high-ranking diplomats and heads of state, the conference also heard from twelve-year-old Canadian environmental activist Severn Cullis-Suzuki. Suzuki had founded an advocacy group called Environmental Children's Organization (ECO). Addressing a plenary session of the conference, Suzuki gave an emotional, blunt, no-holds-barred speech in which she both laid blame on the nations of the world for the current state of the environment and implored them to solve the problem. Early on, she stated, "Coming up here today, I have no hidden agenda. I am fighting for my future. Losing my future is not like losing an election, or a few points on the stock market." Although her tone coming from an adult would be considered shrill and patronizing, she conveyed a sense of genuine concern and passion when she then said, "I'm only a child, yet I know we are all part of a family five billion strong: in fact, 30 million species strong-and borders and governments will never change that." Towards the end of her speech, she then implored the delegates to remember why they were there reminding them, "Do not forget why you are attending these conferences-who you're doing this for. We are your own children. You are deciding what kind of a world we are growing up in." (Suzuki speech) Suzuki's speech had its intended effect and was widely praised by the delegates. It could be argued that long before Swedish climate activist Greta Thunberg harangued the UN about global warming in 2019, Suzuki set the template for child environmental activism with passionate, concerned, demanding, and accusatory, but not quite inflammatory, rhetoric.

Although the conference had lofty ambitions and goals, to many, there seemed to be a division between first world developed countries and third world developing ones. This was apparent when Fidel Castro, Cuba's Communist dictator, addressed the conference. Castro, who was dressed in his standard military uniform, gave one of his trademark ideological speeches where he blamed the environmental problems the conference sought to address on the United States and other developed nations. Castro stated that the developed world, which he referred to as the "consumer society," exploited the resources and energy of the world and that developing nations such as his paid the price, stating they were "Colonies yesterday, nations exploited and looted today by an unfair economic world order." He then went on to urge the world to "Pay the ecological debt, not the external debt," as well as calling on science to help bring about the use of sustainable development that would meet the world's needs and cause no further damage to the environment. (C-SPAN. Castro: Rio) Although Castro's speech reflected what was part and parcel of his long-standing animosity towards the developed world, the United States in particular, he did touch upon a point on which there was major contention between the two sides. This sentiment was echoed by Brazilian Fernando Collor de Mello, who stated, "You can't have an environmentally healthy planet in a world that is socially unjust." (Time, 1992) Developing countries sought to modernize as their populations grew, and as a result, they became more industrialized.

Developed countries stressed the necessity of conservation, particularly in regards to the Brazilian rainforest. This divide came to be known as the North bloc of nations, which comprised North America, Europe, and Japan, vs. the South bloc made up of Asia, Africa, Central, and South America. Both sides accused the other of hypocrisy. The South bloc, while blaming the North for the deterioration of the global environment due to their lifestyle of consumerism, sought that very same lifestyle in order to raise their standard of living. The North bloc, whose countries already had the highest standard of living on the planet, wanted South bloc countries to rein in the development of their forests in tropical regions. The South then countered that these restrictions should also apply to temperate, or boreal, forests in the northern hemisphere. This was almost certainly a swipe at the United States, whose logging practices in the Pacific Northwest harvested a large amount of these trees, many of them ancient forests that also served as carbon sinks, whereby they absorb Carbon Dioxide (CO_2) gas from the atmosphere. Due to the forest's economic importance, the United States had refused to even consider scaling back logging in the region. (Time, 1992) An intractable impasse had been reached.

Over the eleven-day period of the conference, the delegates hammered out a number of agreements regarding the protection of the oceans, forests, and wildlife. The United States caused a stir when, much to the chagrin and embarrassment of William Reilly, Administrator of the EPA, President Bush refused to sign the much-vaunted Convention on Biological Diversity. British Prime Minister John Major was certainly not alone when he called on the United States to take leadership on the environmental crisis, as the United States was responsible for 23% of CO_2 emissions planet wide, as many other countries had also expected Americans to lead. (Gore, p.176.1992) However, like all powerful nations, the United States had its own set of concerns and issues that often did not align with the rest of the world. The treaty required all signatories to share technology in order to help preserve Earth's ecosystems as well as genetic resources from plants and animals. The President's main concern was that the treaty did not provide adequate protections for American companies' intellectual property rights. In light of the continuing recession, American industry and business were also resistant to any new regulations that might cost jobs or slow production. This was a concern that the President was especially sensitive to in an election year. Despite the push back over the refusal to be a party to the treaty, the President and his team still tried to put the best possible spin on the conference as they could, citing other agreements they could get behind.

One such agreement was the ambitious and detailed Agenda 21, which was a blueprint for nations and localities to implement environmentally friendly policies and technologies in order to combat climate change as well as alleviate poverty. Agenda 21 contained a long list of initiatives that the summit nations resolved to address together. These issues ranged from changing global consumption patterns, management of biotechnology, and protection of freshwater supplies etc. Each proposal was broken into the following sections: 1. Basis for Action. 2. Activities 3. Objective 4. Data and Information 5. International and Regional Cooperation and Coordination 6. Means of Implementation. Perhaps most importantly, each proposal had an estimated cost of implementation, which varied widely. For example, the cost of addressing the issue of transporting hazardous waste and dumping was estimated at $18.5 billion per annum for the period of 1993-2000 (A-21, p.202, 1993) while the management of toxic chemicals was only estimated at $10 million for the same period (A-21, p. 191. 1993). As detailed as these estimates were, they had not been reviewed by the nations that had to implement them, and as such, were quite broad, as Secretariat Strong conceded. Agenda 21 also sought to provide for the transfer of cutting-edge, environmentally friendly technology to less wealthy nations. This would be a crucial step towards reducing CO_2 emissions as developing countries tend to rely more on fossil fuels for their energy needs and would involve both the public and private sectors working together in tandem. Predictably, a major issue of contention arose between oil-producing nations in the Middle East and the conference's proposals to cut back on fossil fuels. As with the issue of deforestation in the developing world and developed countries, the conference would have to find some sort of compromise to satisfy both parties. Thus, section 3.2 of chapter 3, Combating Poverty in Agenda 21, acknowledged that it must be taken into account that a significant amount of the population depends on the production of fossil fuels for their livelihoods. Despite all the legalities of implementations and costs involved, for the first time, a comprehensive plan of action was being adopted by a majority of the world's nations in order to address current and future issues relating to climate change, even if it was non-binding.

Although getting 178 nations together for an international conference of major significance was an accomplishment in and of itself, the likelihood that any legally binding treaty could be unanimously agreed upon and ensure the participation of the United States was remote. What all parties were able to agree upon was a set of twenty-seven principles that would serve as guidelines for future environmental policy going forward, which would be called the Rio Declaration. Principle #1 of the declaration stated, "Human beings are at the center of concerns for sustainable development. They are entitled to a healthy and productive life in harmony with nature. Many of the principles were common sense, such as women having full participation in the affairs of state or nations being required to notify each other in case of a natural disaster that could impact their neighbors. However, one principle stood out as a means of holding nations accountable for pollution and environmental disasters. Principle #16 of the declaration stated that, "National authorities should endeavor to promote the internationalization of environmental costs and the use of economic instruments, taking into account the approach that the polluter should, in principle, bear the cost of pollution, with due regard to the public interest and without distorting international trade and investment." Had Agenda 21 been a legally binding agreement with teeth, then this principle certainly could have made a difference by making corporations and states think twice before they engage in activities harmful to the environment. As watered down as the language of the declaration was, it still served its purpose as a foundation of principles moving forward.

With both North and South Bloc countries literally at loggerheads (no pun intended) over the issue of development regarding the world's forests, it was seen as virtually impossible for any sort of binding agreement to be crafted, let alone signed, between the parties. A report on the conference published by the government of Canada cut right to the heart of the impasse when it stated, "In the end, the UNCED negotiations came down to a matter of money. The industrialized nations have it, and the developing countries want it. If the industrialized nations want environmental protection, they must be prepared to pay for it. The tensions between rich and poor and the financial conflicts that underlie them were at the heart of every major negotiation." (Meakin, 1992) As with Agenda 21, the best that both sides could hope to accomplish was a statement of principles and a series of guidelines going forward. What emerged was the Authoritative Statement of Principles for a Global Consensus on the Management, Conservation and Sustainable Development of All Types of Forests, or to put it simply, The Forest Principles. Many of the principles skirted language that could cause any division among the signatories and was fairly innocuous. Principle 1 (a) stated that nations have the right to exploit their resources in order to meet their economic and political needs provided that they cause no harm to the environment of any neighboring countries. Yet it made no mention of whether the action caused any damage within the country exploiting its resources.

As with the Rio Declaration, Principle 4 (b) encouraged the "full participation of women in all aspects of the management, conservation and sustainable development of forests should be actively promoted." The document then went on to urge that nations should seek to find ways of reducing pollutants released due to logging and not restricting trade of lumber in order to aid in conservation efforts. Exchanges of technologies and research in regard to forest management were also mentioned. Principle (15) closed by stating, "Pollutants, particularly air-borne pollutants, including those responsible for acidic deposition, that are harmful to the health of forest ecosystems at the local, national, regional and global levels should be controlled." (UN.org) As with Agenda 21, it was up to the individual nations as to whether they would follow these guidelines. Despite the fact that it was non-binding, the Forest Principles still marked a significant benchmark in terms of the nations of the world recognizing the importance of preserving and managing the forests for future generations.

The most lasting accomplishment of the conference was the establishment of the United Nations Framework Convention on Climate Change (UNFCCC). A product of the UN's Intergovernmental Panel on Climate Change (IPCC) report issued in 1990, the convention had already been drafted by the time the Earth Summit took place and was awaiting signatures of countries willing to join. Signed by 154 nations in attendance, the convention would provide a forum for nations to consult one another on how to combat climate change as well as forge international agreements going forward. The UNFCCC consisted of twenty-six articles ranging from addressing issues of sustainability, the sharing of research, technology, and finances, etc.

The convention's decision-making body would be called the Conference of the Parties. A Secretariat of the Convention was established along with a means to resolve disputes and propose new amendments. Article #2 defined the objective of the convention as," the stabilization of greenhouse gas concentrations in the environment at a level that would prevent dangerous anthropogenic interference with the climate system.

Such a level should be achieved within a time frame sufficient to allow ecosystems to adapt naturally to climate change, to ensure that food production is not threatened, and to enable economic development to proceed in a sustainable manner." Article #4 was a lengthy section detailing commitments each member state was to be responsible for. Of note was how both Articles 8&9 emphasized the needs of developing countries in regard to funding, research, and the transfer of technology. Since the convention framework was non-binding, countries had no legal obligation to live up to their commitments, which, like the other agreements made, would prove problematic.

Although it was not legally binding, UNFCCC would in time provide the impetus for such landmark agreements such as the 1997 Kyoto Protocol and the 2015 Paris Climate Accords. Both agreements would be aimed at reducing greenhouse gases and mitigating the effects of climate change. As with the Convention on Biodiversity, the two treaties would have to contend with a United States that, at times, was not willing to commit and be a party to them. In the case of Kyoto, the U.S. Senate refused to ratify the treaty, whereas with the Paris Accords, the U.S. initially joined under President Obama in 2015 only to withdraw under President Trump in 2020. Upon taking office in 2021, President Biden rejoined the agreement with Trump, then subsequently once again withdrew when he regained the Presidency in 2025.

The Earth Summit in Rio de Janeiro demonstrated that global environmental concerns were becoming widespread in several areas of national policy. It also showed how climate change was an issue that did not recognize national borders and was something nations would have to cooperate on to address. A major example of this would be the North American Free Trade Agreement (NAFTA). Trade among the three nations of North America (The United States, Canada, and Mexico) had long been an issue between them. In 1988, US President Ronald Reagan and Canadian Prime Minister Brian Mulroney signed a bilateral trade deal that would eliminate tariffs and trade restrictions on goods flowing between the two countries as well as foster investment. Despite strong liberal opposition in Canada, the agreement passed after Prime Minister Mulroney's coalition won a governing majority in the 1988 election.

Upon coming to office, President George H.W. Bush began negotiations with Mexican President Carlos Salinas de Gortari for a similar trade deal in 1990. Not wanting to lose the gains made from the US-Canada deal, Prime Minister Mulroney was allowed to become a party to the talks and make it a three-way deal. With negotiations finally concluded, the deal was signed in San Antonio, Texas on October 7, 1992, with President Bush, President Salinas, and Prime Minister Mulroney in attendance. NAFTA became a polarizing issue in both the US and Canada, while less so in Mexico. As stated previously, it particularly drew the ire of third-party candidate H. Ross Perot, who was dead set against it while Bill Clinton straddled both sides. Opposition from Labor and environmentalist groups was particularly vehement. Import and export tariffs levied in one country on any given item could have a wide range of effects in other countries, ranging from wages paid to the workers who produced the goods, to the health of the industry itself. The cost of labor also plays a major role in whether a company decides to outsource their operations and jobs overseas, along with environmental laws and regulations in the host country. Protective tariffs also served the purpose of helping to protect a nation's specific industries from foreign competition.

Perot's objection to the treaty was so great that he even wrote an entire book about it to support his arguments, Save Your Job, Save Our Country: Why NAFTA Must be Stopped-Now!. One of Perot's main issues with the treaty was that President Bush, like President Reagan in 1988, was granted what was called fast-track authority by Congress in 1991 to negotiate the trade deal with zero input from lawmakers. To him, this was unfair and undemocratic. (Perot, 24-25, 1993). Also, like many environmentalists, Perot voiced concerns that there were not strong enough protections for the environment, particularly in Mexico. One example of this is how Mexico's regulations on pesticides for agriculture differed from those of the United States and Canada. The reason for this was that the Mexican government simply did not have adequate funds or technology to enforce regulations as stringent as their counterparts to the North. (Baer, 82, 1994) Labor's main concern, as well as Perot's, was that American and Canadian companies would leave their respective countries and set up shop in Mexico, where they could pay their workers much lower wages. Also, their workforce would not have the same environmental and union protections.

Another question was how beneficial the deal would be for America, given the fact that her economy and GDP were so much larger than that of Canada and Mexico. To some, it seemed that the benefits would be cheaper goods for Americans at the expense of job losses. Upon assuming the Presidency in January 1993, Bill Clinton pushed hard for ratification of the treaty and even enlisted the help of former Presidents Ford, Carter, and Bush to lobby for its passage in Congress. As the debate unfolded, it was clear that President Clinton was having to fight against his own liberal base in the Democratic Party, particularly organized labor and the unions they represented. The debate in Congress was particularly acrimonious, with President Clinton in the strange position of working with Republicans to ensure passage. In order to assuage critics of the treaty, President Clinton added the North American Agreement on Labor Cooperation and the North American Agreement on Environmental

Cooperation to ensure that all parties would adhere to the same regulations. The treaty would also give significant protection to each country's trade secrets and proprietary information. (Hufbauer. 89. 1993) Still, a high-profile push was needed to sway public opinion ahead of the congressional vote.

On November 9, 1993, Vice President Al Gore and Ross Perot participated in a debate on Larry King's cable TV show, Larry King Live, on CNN. The congressional vote on the controversial trade treaty was six days away, and the debate could have enormous consequences for the prospects of final passage. Vice President Al Gore, who had a deserved reputation as a policy wonk, much as his boss, President Bill Clinton, was widely expected to thrash the venerable yet wily Perot. At the start of the debate, Vice President Al Gore told of a man he knew from Tennessee who made tires for a living and how his company would benefit from NAFTA, as lower tariffs would allow his company's tires to be sold in Mexico. He then chided Perot with a framed picture of Senator Reed Smoot and Rep. Willis Hawley, the authors of the notorious Smoot-Hawley Tariff Act of 1930, which worsened the Great Depression, as well as calling the deal "even–Stephen" in terms of how much each country would benefit. Perot, as usual, had plenty of charts to back up his arguments, but Gore did also. The debate itself was filled with plenty of personal attacks and constant interruptions. When Perot claimed that the entire effort to push the agreement through Congress was the work of "highly paid lobbyists", Gore then countered that Perot himself had lobbied the powerful House Ways and Means Committee back in the 1970s to give a tax break to his business. Perot then accused the Vice President of lying. When Perot was trying to deny a claim that was made by the Vice President, and Gore continued to interrupt him, Perot shot back, "Let's try to have an unnatural event and not interrupt me."

To anyone watching the debate, the result could not have been clearer. The Vice President, policy wonk and ardent environmentalist, had easily humbled the Perot colossus and deflated several of his claims. On policy and points, Gore was largely declared the winner, and although the general public's view of NAFTA improved dramatically, the real audience was the undecided members of Congress who would decide the treaty's fate. A week later, on November 17, the treaty passed in the House of Representatives 234-200, with the Senate following suit three days later, 61-38. It's quite telling that out of all the Nay votes, twenty-eight were Democrats in the Senate and 156 in the House. (Congress.gov) The treaty then became effective on January 1, 1994. Just one year later, the World Trade Organization (WTO) was founded on January 1, 1995 pursuant to the Marrakesh Agreement of April 1994, which replaced the General Agreement on Trade and Tariffs (GATT). The WTO is the largest trade organization in the world and has over 160 members. In many aspects, the organization seeks to accomplish on a global scale what NAFTA did between Canada, the United States, and Mexico.

Perhaps no more controversial pieces of economic legislation arose during the early 1990s than the NAFTA treaty. As such, the results of NAFTA have been a mixed bag over the years. US industries were hard hit as they relocated to Mexico, while at the same time, consumers enjoyed access to cheaper goods from Canada and Mexico. Over the coming years, the treaty would be attacked from both the left and the right, with President Donald Trump renegotiating certain terms of the agreement throughout 2017-2018 and ultimately replacing it with the United States-Mexico Canada Agreement (USMCA), which became effective in 2020. USMCA provides more up to date regulations and protections on commerce conducted digitally over the internet. Like the Earth Summit in Rio, international trade, NAFTA in particular, demonstrated that the world was becoming increasingly interconnected and interdependent. The issues of climate change and global warming are even more important now than they were thirty-three years ago in 1992, as the ever-increasing ferocity of natural disasters such as hurricanes and wildfires demonstrate. Although these issues are still paramount and have yet to be solved conclusively, the conversation about how to do so began in 1992 and still goes on.

Of all the events that made headlines and captured the world's imagination throughout the year, one of the most spectacular occurred in the realm of sports. A little over a month after the end of the Rio Earth Summit, the 1992 Summer Olympics opened in Barcelona, Spain, from July 25 - August 9. Due to an April 1989 decision made by the International Amateur Basketball Federation, players from the National Basketball Association (NBA) would be allowed to participate in the 1992 Olympics. Everyone knew this applied only to the United States, and in some quarters, there was alarm that this would make the games too one-sided and give them a grossly unfair monopoly. These concerns turned out to be very real as what became known as the Dream Team utterly dominated all the teams they played and easily won the gold medal. Coached by Chuck Daly, the team roster was nothing short of legendary. It consisted of: Larry Bird, Magic Johnson, David Robinson, Patrick Ewing, Scottie Pippen, Clyde Drexler, Karl Malone, John Stockton, Christopher Mullin, Charles Barkley, Christian Laettner, and last but certainly not least, Michael Jordan.

Instead of grumbling over the massive advantage the US team had, it turned out that all the other participants were excited to just share the court with the Dream Team, regardless of how badly they lost. And lose they did. The closest game was against Croatia, 103-70 while the largest winning margin came against Cuba, 137-57. To see the team in action was nothing short of simply magic (pun intended). To watch any of the games was to be treated to a non-stop spectacle of three-point shots, lay-ups, alley oops culminating in a never-ending supply of slam dunks. The Dream Team finished the games with an astounding record of: W: 8 L: 0 Points For: 938, Points Allowed: 588. (Wallenchinsky.p.268-269. 1996) Of note was that a newly independent Lithuania won the Bronze medal in a rematch with the Russian Federation 82-78. Ironically, just four years earlier in 1988, players from both teams had been teammates when playing for the U.S.S.R.

Women made several major advances and gains throughout 1992. One of the most significant was when the Anglican Church Synod in the United Kingdom voted on November 11, 1992, by just two votes to allow women to be ordained as Priests in the Church for the first time after Australia and South Africa followed suit earlier in the year. This change came about after years of debate over doctrine and the proper place of women in the church hierarchy. It also represented a major victory for women's rights in one of the most conservative facets of society. Although there remains fierce opposition from several quarters, the number of women priests has risen steadily over the past thirty years since the first ordinations took place in 1994. As of 2024, women comprise 33.5% of all paid clergy within the Anglican Church of England. Out of 6,715 full-time clergy, 2,148 are women. (Saintgeorgesmalaga.com/ 2024)

Perhaps the greatest individual accomplishment of the year occurred on September 12, 1992, when the Space Shuttle Endeavor carried thirty-five-year-old Mae C. Jemison into space with STS-47 (Space Transportation System) along with six other astronauts, making her the first African American woman in space. Born on October 17, 1956, in Decatur, Alabama as the youngest of three children, Jemison showed an interest in science and outer space and an independence of spirit and will typical of most trailblazers. When she was in elementary school, her teacher thought she was joking when her reply to what she wanted to do when she grew up was to be a scientist. A gifted student, she enrolled in high school at twelve and Stanford at just sixteen. While an undergrad at Stanford, Jemison had to deal with casual attitudes of sexism and racism from fellow students and professors alike. She also had to deal with people not taking her seriously because of her age. Despite all this, she excelled and decided to apply for medical school at Cornell University in New York. After attending and graduating from Cornell, Dr. Jemison worked as a Doctor with the Peace Corps in West Africa. Having been inspired by astronauts Guion Bluford and Sally Ride and her childhood experiences of watching Lieutenant Uhura on Star Trek: The Original Series, Jemison then applied to be an astronaut with the National Aeronautics and Space Administration (NASA) in 1985. After the Challenger disaster in January 1986, NASA postponed hiring any new astronauts for a year. In June 1987, she found out she was one of fifteen selected out of a pool of 100 interviewed out of 2,000 applicants. (Jemison. p. 170. 2021)

After completion of her training at NASA, Dr. Jemison was slated for the STS-47 launch aboard the Space Shuttle Endeavour on September 12, 1992. In addition to Dr. Mae, the crew of STS-47 would also have the first married couple (Mark C. Lee and Jan Davis) and the first Japanese astronaut (Mamoru Mohri). Upon reaching orbit, she conducted several experiments involving reproduction in the zero-gravity environment of space. One of which involved fertilizing eggs from four female South African clawed frogs, which then spawned 100 tadpoles three days later. (Gibson. 145-146. 2014) Another experiment centered on how to combat space and motion sickness via biofeedback techniques that many astronauts suffered from during their missions. Space Shuttle Endeavour returned to Earth on September 20, 1992, successfully completing its mission.

For someone who loved and was inspired by Star Trek so much, Dr. Jemison would go on to guest star in the episode "Second Chances" of Star Trek: The Next Generation which aired on May 24, 1993. Less than four months after the flight of STS-47, a new series of Star Trek, Deep Space Nine, would air on January 3, 1993, and feature Avery Brooks as Commander Benjamin Sisko, the first African American lead in the genre. Two years later, Kate Mulgrew would star as Captain Kathryn Janeway in Star Trek: Voyager, making her the first female Captain lead in a series. No doubt these were developments that pleased Dr. Jemison a great deal. Dr. Jemison resigned from NASA in 1993 and then taught at Dartmouth University. She then went on to found the Dorothy Jemison Foundation for Excellence in 1994, which was named after her mother. The foundation serves a variety of purposes, from sponsoring summer camps to essay competitions. Dr. Jemison continues to reach for the stars. Literally. In 2011, her foundation was awarded a $500,000 grant to help facilitate what is called the 100 Year Starship project, which seeks to make travel to the nearest star possible within a century, as well as for humans to journey deeper into space. The project is ongoing with symposiums being held every couple of years to discuss theories, physics, and potential technologies. Dr. Jemison's flight in space was the culmination of a lifetime of hard work, dedication, and refusing to let others define what her place in life should be. As she once said, "Don't be limited by others' limited imaginations." (Gibson. p. 147. 2014) On September 12, 1992, she showed the world where that mindset can lead a person to chase their dreams.

On October 7, 1992, the U.S, Canada, and Mexico signed the NAFTA (North American Free Trade Agreement) in San Antonio, Texas. Along with the Rio Earth Summit, NAFTA showed how interconnected and interdependent the world was becoming.

A lifelong dream realized. Dr. Mae C. Jemison becomes the first African American female in space along with Mamoru Mohri, the first Japanese astronaut in space, on STS-47, abroad Space Shuttle Endeavour, which launched September 12, 1992.

Earth Summit: Rio de Janeiro, June 3 - 14, 1992. The conference sought to form a global consensus on how to deal with Climate Change with mixed results.

Afterwards

In his 2012 book 1775: A Good Year for Revolution, Kevin Phillips argues that 1775 was a "long" year in the sense that the events that occurred during it had their roots long before it occurred. The same holds true for events that came about in the immediate aftermath of 1775, most notably the July 4, 1776, Declaration of Independence. In many ways, 1992 was indeed a very long year. The populism of billionaire Ross Perot made possible the rise of Donald Trump, who, unlike Perot, would obtain the Presidency and have a cultural and political effect far more profound than that of Perot's.

The chaos and disorder of the Russian Federation's attempt to become a liberal democracy under Boris Yeltsin in 1992 led directly to the current oligarchy of Vladimir Putin with all its subsequent authoritarianism. The roots of the rage and violence that engulfed Los Angeles in April 1992 cannot fully be understood without a close look at the long history of discrimination and racism in America. The legacy of police brutality is still with us, as the murder of George Floyd in May 2020 shows all too well. Likewise, it is not possible to understand the explosion, resonance, and popularity of Grunge without a thorough understanding of the musical landscape in the 1980's nor the brutality of the Bosnian war without a full understanding of the ethnic, cultural and religious divisions that boiled to the surface just after the collapse of Yugoslavia. The attempt to address climate change/global warming via such agreements as the 2015 Paris Climate Accords and the development of renewable energy are a direct result of the United Nations Framework Convention on Climate Change (UNFCCC) that was established at the Rio Earth Summit in 1992.

It could be said that all history is interconnected and that to understand 1992 and why it is so significant, it is necessary to delve into events that happened before and after that year. After all, as this book has made clear, at least I hope, the world we now live in is the world that began with the events of 1992.

Matthew R. Smith
January 26, 2025
Cary, North Carolina

Bibliography

American Rhetoric Online Speech Bank. Severn Suzuki: "Speech at UN Conference on Environment and Development." [https://www.americanrhetoric.com/speeches/severnsuzukiunearthsummit.htm] 11. January 2025.

Aron, Leon. <u>Yeltsin: A Revolutionary Life</u>. St. Martin's Press: New York, 2000.

Aslund, Anders. "Russia and the International Financial Institutions." *Carnegie Endowment for International Peace*. 18. January 2000. [https://carnegieendowment.org/posts/2000/01/russia-and-the-international- financial-institutions?lang=en] 30. September 2024.

Azerrad, Michael. <u>Come As You Are: The Story Of Nirvana</u>. Broadway Books: New York, 1993.

Baer, Delal M. & Weintraub, Sidney. <u>The NAFTA Debate: Grappling with Unconventional Trade Issues.</u> Lynne Rienner Publishers: London, 1994.

Baldassare, Mark. <u>The Los Angeles Riots: Lessons for the Urban Future.</u> Westview Press: San Francisco, 1994.

Baltin, Steve. (2020, November.1) "Thirty Years Later How Rock the Vote Changed Music and Politics." *Forbes Magazine*. [https://www.forbes.com/sites/stevebaltin/2020/11/01/thirty-years-later-how-rock- the-vote-changed-music-and-politics/] 2024. June 24.

Blumenthal, Sidney. <u>The Clinton Wars</u>. Plume and Penguin Ltd: London, 2003.

Bognanno, Mario F. & Ready, Kathryn J. The North American Free Trade Agreement: Labor, Industry, and Government Perspectives. Quorum Books: Westport, CT& London, 1993.

Bowden, Mark. Black Hawk Down. Penguin Publishing Group: New York, 1999.

Burns, John F. (1992. July. 4) "U.N. Airlift to Sarajevo Hits Full Stride." *The New York Times.* [https://www.nytimes.com/1992/07/04/world/un-airlift-to-sarajevo-hits-full-stride.html] 22. June 2024.

Bush, George. All The Best: My Life in Letters and Other Writings. Scribner: New York, 1999.

Bush, George and Scowcroft, Brent. A World Transformed. Alfred A. Knopf: New York, 1998.

Cannon, Lou. Official Negligence: How Rodney King and The Riots Changed Los Angeles and the LAPD. Times Books and Random House: New York, 1997.

Carville, James. "The Clinton Years.": *Frontline: Nightline:* PBS. January 2001 [https://www.pbs.org/wgbh/pages/frontline/shows/clinton/interviews/carville.html] 27. May 2024.

Carville, James and Matalin, Mary with Knobler, Peter: All's Fair: Love, War and Running for President. Random House: New York, 1994.

Ching, Jacqueline. Genocide in Modern Times: Genocide and The Bosnian War. The Rosen Publishing Group: New York, 2009.

Clinton, Bill. My Life. Alfred A. Knopf: New York, 2004.

Clinton, Hillary. <u>Living History: Hillary Rodham Clinton</u>. Simon and Schuster: New York, 2003.

Chollet, D. 2016. July.19. "Obama's Red Line Revisited." *Politico Magazine* [https://www.politico.com/magazine/story/2016/07/obama-syria-foreign-policy-red-line-revisited-214059] 18. July 2024.

Central Intelligence Agency. *Economic Survey of Russia*: 1992. March 1993. [https://www.cia.gov/readingroom/docs/DOC_0000292328.pdf] 17. September 2024.

Congress.gov [https://www.congress.gov/bill/103rd-congress/house-bill/3450/actions] 6. February 2025.

Coll, Steve. <u>Ghost Wars: The Secret History of the CIA, Afghanistan, And Bin Laden, From the Soviet Invasion to September 10, 2001.</u> Penguin: London, 2004.

Colton, Timothy J. <u>Yeltsin: A Life.</u> Basic Books: New York, 2008.

Court TV. Search: Rodney King Trial. [https://www.courttv.com/title/108-ca-v-powell-et-al-prosecution-closing-argument/] 20. November 2024.

Cross. Charles R. <u>Heavier Than Heaven: A Biography of Kurt Cobain. Updated And expanded.</u> Hachette Book Group: New York, 2001, 2019.

Crowe, Cameron. "5 Against the World." *Rolling Stone*. Issue.668. October 28, 1993.

C-SPAN. [https://www.c-span.org/program/united-nations/earth-summit-opening-plenary-part-2/19386] 11. January 2025.

Dallaire, Lieutenant-General Romeo. <u>Shake Hands with The Devil: The Failure of Humanity in Rwanda.</u> Random House: Canada, 2003.

Duncan. 2020, 23. February 2020. *Ross Perot Campaign Commercial: Chicken Feathers, Deep Voodoo and the American Dream* [Video] (You Tube) [https://youtu.be/tm8_Cn4M9wc?si=al4V_cSjuPLuf63x].

Earth Summit 92. The United Nations Conference on Environment and Development: Rio de Janeiro, 1992. Regency Press Corporation: United Kingdom,1992.

Ellison, J Herbert. Boris. Yeltsin and Russia's Democratic Transformation. University of Washington Press: Seattle, 2006.

Feb 3. 2022. "Bosnia and Herzegovina marks 30th anniversary of Independence." *Euronews*. [https://www.euronews.com/2022/03/01/bosnia-herzegovina-marks-30th-anniversary-of-independence. Feb. 3, 2022]. 25. June 2024.

Fogelson, Robert M. Mass Violence in America: The Los Angeles Riots. Arno Press & The New York Times: New York, 1969.

Fukuyama, Francis. The End of History and The Last Man Standing. Free Press: New York, 1992

Gaddis, John Lewis. The Cold War: A New History. Penguin Books: New York, 2005.

Gale, Dennis E. Understanding Urban Unrest: From Reverend King to Rodney King. Sage Publications: London, 1996.

Gibson, Karen Bush. Women in Space: 23 Stories of First Flights, Scientific Missions, and Gravity-Breaking Adventures. Chicago Review Press: Chicago, 2014.

Glenny, Misha. The Balkans: Nationalism, War, and The Great Powers, 1804-1999. Penguin Putnam: New York, 2000.

Goldberg, Danny. <u>Serving The Servant: Remembering Kurt Cobain.</u> Harper Collins: New York, 2019.

Goldman, Marshall L. <u>Lost Opportunity: Why Economic Reforms in Russia Have Not Worked.</u> W.W. Norton & Company: New York, 1994.

Gore, Senator Al. <u>Earth in the Balance: Ecology and the Human Spirit.</u> Houghton Mifflin Company: Boston, 1992.

Gustafson, Thane. <u>Capitalism Russian-Style.</u> University Press: Cambridge, 1999.

Grieder, William. "After South Central: The White Conscience." *Rolling Stone*. Issue 633. June 25, 1992.

Hamilton, Nigel. <u>Bill Clinton: An American Journey: Great Expectations.</u> Random House: New York, 2003.

Hamilton, Nigel. Bill Clinton: <u>Mastering the Presidency.</u> Public Affairs: New York, 2007.

Harrison, Lavelle and Thomas, Armin.1. April 2023. "Examining Ross Perot's Impact on the 1992 Presidential Election Results." *Split-Ticket*. [https://splitticket.org/2023/04/01/examining-ross-perots-impact-on-the-1992-presidential-election/] 7. July 2024.

Hufbauer, Gary Clyde and Schott, Jefferey J<u>. NAFTA: An Assessment.</u> Institute for International Economics: Washington, D.C., 1993.

Hufbauer, Gary Clyde and Schott, Jefferey J. <u>NAFTA Revisited: Achievements and Challenges.</u> Institute for International Economics: Washington D.C., 2005.

International Monetary Fund. Russian Federation Outstanding Purchases and Loans From January 1, 1992, to December 31, 1992. [https://www.imf.org/external/np/fin/tad/extcredt1.aspx?memberKey1=819&date1key=1998-12-31&dateyear=1992-12-31&roption=M] 30. September. 2024.

Jemison, Dr. Mae C. Find Where the Wind Goes: Moments from My Life. Signal Hill Publishing. LLC. 2021.

King, Rodney G. The Riot Within: My Journey from Rebellion to Redemption. Harper One: San Francisco, 2012.

Koon. Sgt. Stacey C. Presumed Guilty: The Tragedy of The Rodney King Affair. Regnery Gateway Publishing: Washington D.C., 1992.

Kornacki, Steve. The Red and The Blue: The 1990's And the Birth of Political Tribalism. Harper Collins: New York, 2018.

National Geographic. "LA 92" 2017. [https://youtu.be/uaotkHlHJwo?si=3qQPZNHTzPDJNqjt] 1. Dec 2024.

Lane, Charles & Writers and Editors of the New Republic. The Black Book of Bosnia: The Consequences of Appeasement. Basic Books: New York, 1996.

Little, Alan & Silber Laura. The Death of Yugoslavia. London: Penguin Books, 1995.

Leip, David. 2004. *Dave Leip's Atlas of Presidential Election.* <https://uselectionatlas.org/RESULTS> 20. May 2024

Magas, Branka & Zanic, Ivo. The War in Croatia and Bosnia-Herzegovina. Frank Cass: London, 2001.

Marks, Craig. "Let's Get Lost." *SPIN*. Vol.10 Iss.10. January 1995.

Meacham, Jon. Destiny and Power: <u>The American Odyssey of George Herbert Walker Bush.</u> Random House: New York, 2015.

Meakin, Stephanie. The Rio Earth Summit: Summary of The United Nations Conference on Environment and Development. [https://publications.gc.ca/Pilot/LoPBdP/BP/bp317-e.htm] Government of Canada Publications: Ottawa, 1992.

Meisler, Stanley. 1993, June 3) "U.N. Refuses to Lift Bosnia Arms Embargo." *The Los Angeles Times.* [https://www.latimes.com/archives/la-xpm-1993-06-30-mn-8607-story.html] 21. June 2024.

"Mikhail Gorbachev's Resignation Speech," World History Commons, https://worldhistorycommons.org/mikhail-gorbachevs-resignation-speech. 14. August 2024.

Mickelthwait, John and Woolridge, Adrian. <u>The Right Nation: Conservative Power in America.</u> Penguin: New York, 2004.

Miller, Zell. <u>A National Party No More: The Conscience of a Conservative Democrat.</u> Stout & Hall Publishers: Atlanta, 2003.

Mitchell, John L. "The Raid That Still Haunts L.A." *The Los Angeles Times.* 14. March 2001. [https://www.latimes.com/archives/la-xpm-2001-mar-14-mn-37553-story.html] 12. October 2024.

Moran, Robert T. & Abbott, Jeffery. <u>NAFTA: Managing Cultural Differences.</u> Gulf Publishing Company: Houston, 1994.

Morrell, Brad. <u>Pearl Jam: The Illustrated Biography.</u> Omnibus Press: New York, 1993.

Parmet, Herbert S. George Bush: The Life of a Lone Star Yankee. Scribner: New York, 1997.

Phillips, Kevin. 1775: A Good Year for Revolution. Viking Press: New York, 2012.

Perot, Ross. United We Stand How We Can Take Back Our Country: A Plan For the 21st Century. Hyperion: New York, 1992.

Perot, Ross & Choate, Pat. Save Your Job, Save Our Country: Why NAFTA Must Be Stopped- Now! Hyperion: New York, 1993.

Posner, Gerald. Citizen Perot: His Life and Times. Random House: Toronto, 1996.

Reader, Bill. "The Story of Pearl Jam: From A Seattle Basement to the Rock And Roll Hall of Fame." *The Seattle Times*. 13. March 2017. [https://www.seattletimes.com/pacific-nw-magazine/pearl-jams-hall-of-fame-career-began-in-a-seattle-basement/] 17. April 2024.

Recording Industry Association of America. Gold & Platinum Search Engine [https://www.riaa.com/gold-platinum/#search_section] 7. July 2024.

Robert, Maryse. Negotiating NAFTA: Explaining the Outcome in Culture, Textiles, Autos, and Pharmaceuticals. University of Toronto Press: Toronto, 2000.

Rolling Stone Editors. Cobain. Rolling Stone Press: New York, 1994.

Roper Center: "How Groups Voted in 1992." *Roper Center for Public Opinion Research*. [https://ropercenter.cornell.edu/how-groups-voted-1992] 2024. June 24.

Sacco, Joe. The Fixer and Other Stories. Drawn & Quarterly: Canada, 2009.

Saint George's Anglican Chaplaincy Malaga.[https://stgeorgesmalaga.com/so-how-many-clergy-in-the-church-of-england-are-now-women/] 7. February 2025.

Smith, Curt. <u>George H.W. Bush: Character at the Core</u>. Potomac Books: University of Nebraska Press, 2014

Time Magazine Editors, 1992: <u>The Year in Review.</u> Time Books: New York, 1993.

Taubman, William. <u>Gorbachev: His Life and Times</u>. W.W. Norton and Company: New York, 2017.

United Nations. Agenda 21: <u>Programme of Action for Sustainable Development: Rio Declaration on Environment and Development.</u> United Nations Department of Public Information: New York, 1992.

United Nations. Conferences and Sustainable Development. "United Nations Conference on Environment and Development, Rio de Janeiro, Brazil, 3-14 June 1992." [https://www.un.org/en/conferences/environment/rio1992] 6. January 2025.

United Nations: United Nations Peacekeeping: "UNISOM1 Background" [https://peacekeeping.un.org/mission/past/unosom1backgr2.html] 24. June 2024.

United Nations: United Nations Peacekeeping: "UNPROFOR Fact Sheet" [https://peacekeeping.un.org/en/mission/unprofor]:14. June 2024.

United Nations: Security Council Report: "UN Documents for Bosnia and Herzegovina: Security Council Resolutions." [https://www.securitycouncilreport.org/un_documents_type/security-council-resolutions/page/3?ctype=Bosnia+%26amp%3B+Herzegovina&cbtype=bosnia-herzegovina#038;cbtype=bosnia-herzegovina] 15. June 2024.

United States Holocaust Memorial and Museum. July 2013. Background: Bosnia and Herzegovina: 1992-1995: United States Holocaust Memorial and Museum [https://www.ushmm.org/genocide-prevention/countries/bosnia Herzegovina/1992-1995] 25.July. 2024.

Wall, Brenda Ph.D. Rodney King Rebellion: A Psychopolitical Analysis of Racial Despair and Hope. African American Images: Chicago, 1992.

Wallechinsky, David. Sports Illustrated Presents: The Complete Book of The Summer Olympics: 1996 Edition. Little Brown and Company: Boston, 1996.

Williams, Robert Gooding. Reading Rodney King: Reading Urban Uprising. Routledge: London, 1993. (Also, Mike Davis)

Wilkerson, Isabell. The Warmth of Other Suns. Vintage: New York, 2010.

Wines, Michael. February 2, 1992. "Bush and Yeltsin Declare Formal End to Cold War." *The New York Times* https://www.nytimes.com/1992/02/02/world/bush-and-yeltsin-declare-formal-end-to-cold-war-agree-to-exchange- visits.html] 27. August 2024.

Wines, Michael. June 17, 1992. Summit in Washington: "Bush and Yeltsin Agree To Cut Long-Range Atomic Warheads: Scrap Key Land-Based Missiles". *New York Times*. [https://www.nytimes.com/1992/06/17/world/summit-washington-bush-yeltsin-agree-cut-long-range-atomic-warheads-scrap-key.html] 15. September 2024.

Wilson, Samuel. 2. March 2013. *Ross Perot 1992-Balancing the Budget & Reforming Government.* [Video] (You Tube) [https://youtu.be/mPIVI0CbCmg?si=xn-UdARheY06vZ59] 25. June 2024.

Yeltsin, Boris. Translated by Glenny, Michael. Against The Grain: An Autobiography. Summit Books: New York, 1990.

Yeltsin, Boris. Translated by Catherine A. Fitzpatrick. The Struggle for Russia. Belka Publishing Company: Times Books, Random House, New York, 1994.

"Yeltsin's Speech. August 19, 1991". Vancouver Island University. [https://web.viu.ca/davies/H102/Yelstin.speech.1991.htm] 14. August 2024.

Zimmerman, Warren. Origins of a Catastrophe: Yugoslavia and Its Destroyers- America's Last Ambassador Tells What Happened and Why. Times Books: New York, 1996.

1992 Republican Party Presidential Primaries (2024). Wikipedia: The Free Encyclopedia [https://en.wikipedia.org/wiki/1992_Republican_Party_presidential_primaries] 20. May 2024.

www.ingramcontent.com/pod-product-compliance
Lightning Source LLC
Chambersburg PA
CBHW070055080526
44586CB00013B/1062